CLINICAL EDUCATION IN SOMATIC PROCESS

Patterns of Distress

Emotional Insults
and Human Form

Stanley Keleman

edited by Gene Hendrix
drawings by the author

Center Press, Berkeley

© 1989 Stanley Keleman

All Rights Reserved
including the right of reproduction
in whole or in part in any form

Published by Center Press
2045 Francisco Street
Berkeley, California 94709

ISBN 0-934320-13-6

Contents

Introduction	i
Challenges to the Formative Process	1
Sydney: The Crushed Child	18
Sharon: An Encounter with Mortality	22
Somatic-Emotional Breakdown	27
Kevin: The Shock of the Unexpected	40
Melissa: An Adultified Child	43
Somatic-Emotional Procedures to Disorganize an Insult	47
Rigidity and Spasticity	
Pulling Up, Surprise, Dread	
Startle, Surprise and Stiffening	
Conflict and Confusion	
Clinical Philosophy and Practical Insights	57
Joan: Family Illness	64
Jacob: Grief and Despair	67
What Somatic-Emotional Education Means	72

Also by Stanley Keleman

Myth & the Body: A Colloquy with Joseph Campbell (1999)
Love: A Somatic View (1994)
Embodying Experience (1987)
Bonding (1986)
Emotional Anatomy (1985)
In Defense of Heterosexuality (1982)
Somatic Reality (1979)
Your Body Speaks Its Mind (1975)
Living Your Dying (1974)
Human Ground/Sexuality, Self and Survival (1973)
Todtmoos: A Book of Poems (1971)

Introduction

Human existence rests upon the fact of embodiment. Embodiment is, in fact, the terms of a person's existence. Somatic reality is how a person embodies himself, how he lives his embodiment, and how he transforms inner experience into a personal shape. Embodiment is an emotional experience, and emotional experience is bodily.

The commonly held notion of body does not apply to what is now known about human existence. The body is more than an object of consciousness and may be consciousness itself. The body is a process—an alive, subjective process—a living chain of events that manifests itself over time.

A person's somatic shape indicates how his experience has affected him, how it has shaped the way he acts as well as his inner existence. An experience coming from outside or inside organizes a person's shape. A lack of continual care, interest, or intimacy may distort his process and reduce his potentialities.

Human form is a complex process of impulse, feeling, thinking, images, and action projecting and embodying a person's vitality in a transitory yet durable expression. The basic adventure of life is how a person organizes the form of his existence, disorganizes what is no longer relevant, and generates new experience to become the person that he lives and not the person that he imagines he has to be.

In human development, a person organizes an adult and social body while also learning to cope with challenges and threats. Anything that challenges a person's bodily self, either from inside or outside himself, directly affects the basis of his functioning and changes his feeling, thinking, acting, and self-perception. His relationship to himself, others, and nature is distorted or, in the language of this book, his form is insulted.

This book examines the way a person responds from inside himself to challenges and insults, shock, trauma, abuse, and neglect and how these past or present painful feelings and experiences are embodied. These experiences bring about a change in shape, organization, and activity, as well as a change in perception and subjective image. A person's structure, organization, and form is altered; he is less than his Maker's intent, he loses his natural and personal innocence and beauty.

Mental and emotional states have an anatomical basis. Deep emotional and traumatic conflicts may not be resolved satisfactorily until one works somatically. A contracted uterus, abdomen, or brain gives rise to feelings of pain and discomfort, a speeded-up heartbeat to anxiety and expectation, a clenched jaw and narrowed shoulders to self-control. Therapy and insight may not change what has become embedded as a spastic contraction or pattern of behavior—to cry, to freeze, to flee.

People enter somatic work because they have psychological or emotional pain, or because they lack a sense of themselves. They lack an inner order, or a feeling order, and they want to discover it. A person resolves his insult not by figuring it out but by creating new or reorganized action patterns and a re-formed body. To disorganize an insult it is necessary that a person become aware of the layers, structure, and organization of his insult pattern. This pattern can then be reorganized.

This book is based on a series of professional seminars given during 1986. In addition, some clients have written about their own experiences to illustrate various patterns of somatic distortion and how they use somatic principles and exercises to help themselves. I have added my clinical comments to some of these case stories. I have also included some somatic exercises typical of the procedures I use in private practice or public workshops. My books *Emotional Anatomy* and *Embodying Experience* provide a clinical application of how I work with various forms of somatic-emotional insult, how an individual can work with himself, or how someone who works with others may try to proceed.

Challenges to the Formative Process

The self is a a somatic-emotional state. Contact and emotional relationship is generated by the qualities of pulsation, aliveness, vitality, excitation, and feeling, the state of the cells and organs. A key to understanding the formative process lies in the nature of the self. Challenges to this process may come from inside or outside the organism.

The Embodied Self

Creation perpetuates itself by organizing animate shapes, be they single cells or the multicelled human organism. Self-formation, the organization of a personal self, replicates this experience of nature. The personal subjective self ripens and matures just like the physical objective form given by nature. The self is a continuous stream of cognitive and emotional responses seeking to sustain and organize shapes of expression. This means that form is more than an expression of function and is, in fact, a function. This concept is important to the logic of formative psychology.

Self-understanding requires more than introspection; it means being able to connect psychological events with biological process and to embody these experiences, giving them somatic and emotional shape and continuity.

Emotional Anatomy introduced the notion of kinetic and liquid morphology and related this to the image of the beating heart, an organ that continually changes shape yet remains constant. The higher its internal activity, the more it organizes shapes that reflect its function. In response to a demand, the heart enlarges or shrinks; it changes form. This is a simple and observable truth.

In the past, people were warriors, hunters, farmers, and laborers. Their cardiovascular systems, their hearts made intense and immediate responses. Today's economy and society require people who are primarily thinkers and social interactors, a long-term, moderate, sustained use of the heart. In changing the shape of the heart, the function of the human being changes. He changes the way he thinks and feels about his own responsiveness. Change in the shape of the heart equals change in its function, change in one's feeling and thinking equals change in the human shape.

Formative psychology tries to understand the shape a person has; how it is organized; how this form functions; what roles it gives rise to; its emotional and neural muscular rules; how vitality and intensity are maintained; and the pattern of insults that has resulted in the form or roles observed. Psychological associations, feelings, interactions, and muscular connections are all part of making a personal shape. In somatic-emotional terms, human shape has both a universal and a personal meaning. Each person is an ontological and universal mammal as well as a particular, personalized one.

A somatic-emotional therapist can make generalizations about a person's shape (overbound, rigid, depressed). The specifics of what a shape means emerge only from a person's history and experiences. Every person goes from embryo to fetus to infant to child to adolescent to adult; he takes those shapes. He has no choice about it. This is an ongoing process that manifests itself and, when it cannot, a person experiences fear, terror, pain, and anxiety. At the same time, every human also organizes a shape that reflects the nature of what society demands of him. Every person has at least two forms. Possibly, if what reflects his personal experience is also present, he has three forms. Shape is the function of growth and living experience. Personality, therefore, is not only how a person functions but how he intends to function.

There can be a discrepancy between one's ability to experience himself and his inability to organize behavior. This discrepancy results in a great deal of personal pain because a person may not be able to bridge his general motility patterns. There is a somatic, emotional, and psychological gap between motility and an ability to organize an action that expresses it. For example, it is commonly said, "Of course, I feel love, but I cannot show it." A person experiences his own motility and aliveness, but has no way to translate them into action.

Challenges and Insults

In forming himself a person meets challenges. He organizes to respond to challenges somewhat as he does to hunger. The model of the immunological system illustrates what a learner the organism is. The organism meets a stranger that it does not know and it immediately calls for help from its companions. Its internal shape changes in terms of numbers and density, and it learns about who this stranger is and how to deal with him. On the way, the immunological system liquifies and ingests the stranger, assimilates his code, and then learns to recognize who he is. This is an analog for how the human meets challenges and forms himself. The forming process stimulates itself through the challenges that it meets in or outside of itself. Challenges, therefore, are food for the organism since they call forth responses from the self that have not existed before. This biological truth, underlying states of mind, is the foundation of a psychology of being. It is a core understanding of formative psychology.

Challenges can become insults. The integrity of a person's process may be unable to sustain itself or to respond. Challenges may become a failure of organization or shape-changing. For example, if, in a person's early life, his parents did not respond as quickly as his hunger demanded, he may have cried louder. The crying pattern has many stages, two of which are crying for help and crying in anger. The person may have received a response to his cries for help, but not to his cries of anger. Thus, he learned how to organize the kind of crying he will engage in. However, if his cries received no response, his crying may have turned into a complaint or a whine of defeat. These involve different expressive shapes or forms, one with an inflated chest, the other with a deflated chest. When shape is insulted, organization and disorganization occur. A person becomes assertive and spastic, or collapses and freezes. Either shape represents an inner structure that gives rise to one's consciousness and behavior, not as words but as feelings and muscle behavior.

If a challenge exceeds a person's ability to respond or if there are painful or intimidating circumstances, he changes his natural shape. Initially, a person responds to an insult with an inherited pattern. As soon as there is an obstacle, one investigates, takes a distance, or immediately attacks it. These investigatory behaviors show that the organism is capable of suspending operations while it organizes its future. There is a relationship between what the organism is doing and a person's psychological and emotional state. For example, one person says that he has waited until now to grow up while another will say that he has hibernated until the danger was past.

Insult and embarrassment are associated with shame and humiliation. A person shrinks and becomes less than what he is capable of being. The shape that he naturally assumes no longer works. For example, to be compliant, a child diminishes himself and gets smaller. An insult shrinks him from his natural form. This pattern can become crystalized and result in a shrunken shape.

The somatic therapist has to find ways to disorganize structure. This involves more than simply releasing muscle tensions. While such release may help, it will fail if the whole shrinking pattern of the client is not disorganized. It is one thing to talk about being humiliated or for a client to cry or to become angry and have associations that accompany these feelings in hopes of releasing this pattern of humiliation. Often, this does not happen. The client has to learn how to disorganize and reorganize his muscular emotional pattern. A somatic therapist may temporarily disorganize an emotional blockage and the client may feel better or have an urge to behave differently, but does not know how to form appropriate behavior. This lack of organismic know-how becomes a secondary insult. The client concludes that it is better to shrink himself because this, at least, is predictable. To the extent that he cannot sustain new behavior, he avoids the pain of being liberated and falls back into shrinking.

The Four Types of Insults

Personal distress and somatic insult affect the growing subjective self. The rush of nature to organize a natural body parallels the development of a personal subjective form. The subjective somatic self starts with an inner image, a universal template in the genetic code that organizes a human form. The specific way an individual's soma is shaped gives rise to a personal subjective sense of one's self and the growth of one's independence. For some parents, the growth of this independent subjective form can be threatening and they respond with insults, criticism, humiliation, even physical abuse. These responses insult the personal form, cripple it, and prevent or stifle its development.

As a challenge increases in severity, a person responds in one of several ways. Responses to irritants, injuries, and insults generally follow the four stages of inflammation: pain, redness, heat, and swelling. Insults call for a change in tissue relationship. Redness indicates an increase in organization, heat an increase in activity, swelling an attempt to neutralize an event, and pain is a signal to withdraw. With a severe challenge to which no response is adequate, there is a regression downward to a place where survival occurs on the vegetative level.

The four states of insult can be labeled shock, trauma, abuse, and neglect. Shock freezes shape or creates a shape that is consistent with how the person interprets his existence at that moment. He may faint, get cold, remove blood from his limbs, shut off consciousness, descend to preserve his plasma balances, and so forth. Trauma means a tear, a rupture, a mutilation, immediate tissue damage, and the beginning of pain. Abuse means irritation, long-term inflammation, wearing down, exhaustion. Neglect is atrophy, disuse, a lack of empathy, a lack of human relationship, and indifference to one's physical or emotional needs.

Each response calls forth a change in shape, to freeze, to become active, to increase activity, or to contain activity. Freeze up, stiffen up, thicken up, swell up—this is what occurs. Freezing results in a spastic shape, increased activity in thickened shape, further activity generates heat and swollenness, and, ultimately, containment or collapse. This is the genesis of the rigid, dense, swollen, and collapsed structures described in *Emotional Anatomy*. Freeze the shape, increase the activity; hunker down, make yourself smaller, pull in, get depressed; get apathetic, swell up; unbound, leak out. These are the possible responses to an insult and each involves a change in shape.

A clinical example of how insult affects shape would be a client who resolved conflicts by throwing temper tantrums. This pattern began when he was a child. His demands were met at first with an appropriate response, then the response was withdrawn. This client is unformed and lacks the ability to contain impulses. This leads to increased activity such as rage, anger, tantrums. These are attempts to get a response, the result of his shape breaking apart. His attempts to get the proper response have failed in the past. The client got a response but not the response he wanted. He receives attention or people capitulate, but what he wants is a response that enables him to develop his next level of maturity. That is precisely what he does not get. After awhile, he becomes afraid and unable to change his tantrum response because he does not know how to disorganize it or organize a new way. After realizing his inadequacy, the real project begins, organizing behavior that better serves his needs.

The Startle Continuum

Part of growing up is learning to deal with obstacles. Obstacles that are not dangerous may hurt but do not invoke shock. For example, sometimes a child falls down, hurts himself, and becomes scared. He responds by freezing but his motility remains. His shape changes but then he comes back to what he was before. But imagine an insult that does not go away, a child that is beaten repeatedly. In this situation the child will freeze, stiffen, increase internal pressure, and attempt to wait it out.

The changes an insult produces in a person's shape can be understood by the formula: intensity x duration x repetition. How intense is an event? How long does it last? How often is it repeated? These questions indicate the response. A loud, forceful, frontal confrontation of a small child by a big adult may last only two seconds, but it will cause the child to freeze. Someone will thicken and shrink against the abuse of persistent harping, complaining, and criticism. Violent neglect causes one to freeze up, long-term neglect causes helplessness, hopelessness, apathy, a lack of direction, and a diminished shape.

The response to an insult involves either an increase or a decrease in activity, and leads to shapes that are overbound and underbound. There are four shapes related to the intensity and duration of an insult. Overbound shapes attempt to maintain aggressive attitudes towards the insult either directly or just below the surface. "I won't give in." Underbound shapes surrender aggression and attempt to appease the aggressor by giving in. Figure One shows the continuum of startle responses.

Following birth and for the first few years, patterns of insult first organize in the upper half of the body. Clutching, holding, crying, reaching out are responses that involve the upper half of the body. Anxiety patterns also begin here. At this stage of its development the organism is committed to belly, mouth, head rather than the belly, genitals, and legs which comes later. Every insult, regardless of what it is or when it comes, results in ungrounding the person, that is, he pulls his viscera inwards and upwards, overexcites his brain, and flees into images and/or hyperalertness. In the human structure whatever scares a person also organizes him upwards and takes him away from the ground. The therapeutic implication is that many people have to be taught to maintain their ground by lowering their center of gravity in the face of anxiety.

A state of shock (Figure One) begins with an increase in intensity and moves from disbelief to anesthetization, and, eventually, dissociation. Trauma invokes rage, fear, and pain; it ends in projection and mania which cover a multitude of events from overactivity to hysteria. With abuse comes humiliation, numbness, submission, denial, and the beginning of withdrawal. Finally, with neglect and abandonment, there is unboundness, depression, and apathy. The first part of this chart shows overbound responses and the second part underbound responses. Intensity x duration x repetition determines the degree of insult. The chart shows how the organism mobilizes its responses as best as it can to maintain the shape that it recognizes as itself.

Recently, a man came to me to deal with his reactions to cardiac surgery. He acknowledged his heart attack and surgery but could not accept anything in his lifestyle that might have contributed to his illness. During the Holocaust this man had suffered severe insults and now looked upon his need for help as a mechanical solution to overcome his feelings of weakness. I suggested to him that these feelings

7 / Patterns of Distress

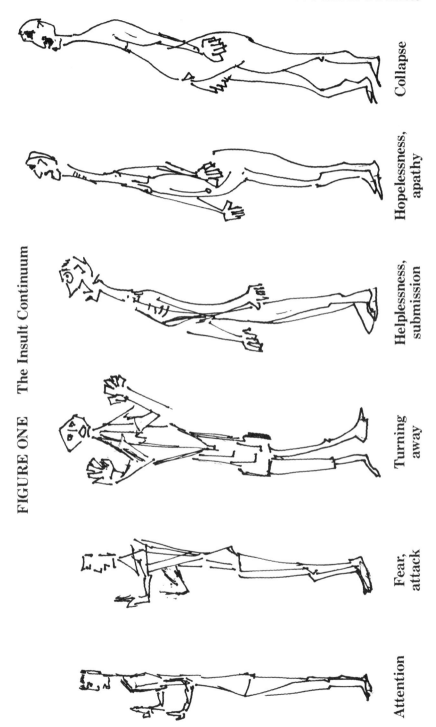

FIGURE ONE The Insult Continuum

Attention · Fear, attack · Turning away · Helplessness, submission · Hopelessness, apathy · Collapse

were his biggest threat. He dared not accept that he felt weak after his operation. He had stabilized himself by densifying and compacting. Fearing defeat or collaspe, he could not let himself disorganize his rigidity.

Differences Among the Startle Positions

A child experiences abuse and abandonment differently. He does not necessarily register as abuse such things as unchanged diapers, prolonged waiting, unregulated and inattentive mealtimes, or frequent babysitting by strangers. But when no one is there for him, a young person knows that he has been abandoned. Abuse is a low-level irritant; a child does not know he is being gradually whittled down. He develops a sub-marginal social personality. There is someone there but also not there.

When abandonment and real neglect occur early, the result is depression, despair, and occasionally death. Institutionalization at an early age can also result in severe problems, among them resignation and a lack of a feeling that one belongs. For a very young child, abandonment, anxiety, and terror go hand in hand and may result in autism. When he is a little older, abuse or humiliation make him shrink and become indifferent to himself or others. Anxiety is experienced as numbness. If he tries to make contact, he does not know what to do. He feels socially awkward.

Shock is a highly intense insult which occurs over a short period of time. For example, someone calls to say that a close friend of yours has died or someone is accidently killed in front of you. When in shock you do not feel anxious or fearful, you do not feel anything. There is disbelief, incomprehension, and numbness.

Trauma is an insult of high intensity but the period may be longer or shorter. For example, a person could be in an accident and his first reaction would be shock not pain. However, as the shock diminishes, pain is experienced. Trauma involves high intensity and possibly short duration, whereas abuse and humiliation involve situations of long duration but mild intensity. Neglect may have little intensity, for example, a child who is ignored over a long period of time.

Abuse is an insult of a persistent interaction with hurtful intent, a parent who constantly criticizes a child or punishes him. Abuse refers to misusing a person or systematically undermining his way of functioning. A parent wants the child to keep his place; every time the child makes a self-assertive statement, he is called "dummy," and punished. Abuse does not necessarily have to be physical. It could be that a child never knows whether he is going to be hit or not. Abuse shrinks the child and generates low self-esteem. This type of insult is different than where a child might drop an expensive dish and find himself harangued, something he usually does not experience.

The difference between shock and trauma is the difference between slapping a child on the behind and punching him in the mouth, or between occasionally shouting at a child and striking him repeatedly. The difference between trauma and abuse is the difference between slapping a child in the face and neglecting to feed him regularly, or accidentally sticking a diaper pin into the baby versus leaving his diapers unchanged until his skin becomes irritated. Trauma involves injury and pain while abuse involves humiliation. Neglect involves physical or emotional abandonment, a state in which the parent ignores or isolates the child.

A person's shape is a combination of genetic givens and the type of insult he has experienced. A young baby lying in a crib will, if insulted, bang his head on the pillow and scream. After he goes through all these convulsions, he may end up in a coma, apathetic and resigned. If, however, a shock is tremendous, he may freeze in place. He will be in danger of dying unless someone keeps him warm, raises his legs, and introduces fluids. There is also moderate shock in which a person goes numb and is full of disbelief. He does not know what happened yet says, "I am all right." As the disbelief wears off he will be filled with grief, rage or tears. At some point, he enters trauma and realizes what is actually occurring.

Shock and trauma and the response of stiffening occur intraspinally, that is, in the spinal and cranial passages and fluids. They affect the intraspinal muscles which regulate the head, neck, limbs, uprightness, and the rotational movements of avoidance and compression. These events happen rapidly and cyclically and they cannot easily be seen, but, in time a behavioral shape appears along with its accompanying feeling.

Responses to Insult

There are two general responses to an insult, the overbound and underbound. In an overbound response the membranes of the structure thicken or stiffen in such a way that the environment cannot be penetrated either from outside-in or inside-out. The membrane acts as a shield to something getting in or getting out. Underbounded structures involve membranes that become unglued; there is porosity in which the world invades the person or he leaks out into the world. If this is relatively mild the underboundedness is weak and the person has some structure to keep the world out or himself in. But if insult is of long duration and the cellular membranes break down, then there is hardly any filter between the person and the world. In these cases there is poor boundary formation.

A response experienced at a particular time becomes internalized as a true cellular state. These responses involve changes in shape as well as changes in the basic feeling state of the organism regardless of what the introjected images are. The brain records what state a person is in and creates an image of it.

Images may contradict one another, for example, one's social image may conflict with his internalized real state. A person may get good grades in school and consider himself smart. Yet these external events actually have little to do with the internal state of a person. For example, a woman who is my client is well-informed, bright, an architect, and a mother. Although she changed her field and received a Ph.D. in clinical psychology, she still suffers from unrelenting feelings of diminished self-worth, anxiety, and incompetence. Her shape is rigid and brittle, with a caved-in chest. When she was nine years old, she was sent to a boarding school where she was lonely, shy, withdrawn and never able to organize a social life so as to gain the contact she needed. She became a clinical psychologist in order to make contact and be wanted. She is an accomplished person who has never overcome the consequences of the insult of abandonment.

On the way to becoming an adult a person runs across devils on the road and responds with vigor and assertion and forms a shape. To understand a person, it is important to know how an insult happened and how old the person was, as well as the intensity and duration of the insult, and how often it was repeated. Insults to a person lock his form in immaturity or overdetermination.

Insults result in four basic responses: structure becomes rigid, dense, swollen, or collapsed. The first response to an insult is to begin to stiffen, to mobilize rigidity in the face of something unknown. If the stakes are slightly higher, the organism stiffens until it becomes spastic. Stiffening is pulling back, bracing the structure in preparation for action; spasticity is stiffening or locking in preparation to receive a blow. Spasticity is like pulling a string taut whereas rigidity braces the organism and thickens it. The difference is in the relationship among an increase in tonus, hypertrophy, and spasticity—three different levels of the same phenomenon. If a shock is very powerful, a person becomes spastic. If there is little structure underneath, the organism may collapse. But if the shock occurs at forty or fifty years of age when there has been experience, the organism will probably not disintegrate.

The relationship between shock, trauma, abuse, and neglect and the different shapes that reflect them are not isolated but exist as part of a continuum. An insult can swing between abuse and neglect or trauma and abuse. For example, as a child grows up a parent may be absent or indifferent, but more present during adolescence. Some parents do not like their children until they get to be self-regulating. So a therapist may find a layer of empathy on top of a layer of unboundedness. The client is kind to others, but unable to distinguish between others and himself. I am describing dissociation, splitting, denial, projection, and depression as somatic-emotional states not simply just states of mind. They are cellular states with psychological implications.

There are differences among stiffening up and pushing away, pulling in and letting nothing out, swelling up, and collapsing. These are all possible responses to an insult—to pull up, to pull back, to pull in, to pull down. It is when these things are carried to an extreme that trouble begins. The state at which a person arrives is related to how strong, how long, and how often his insult occurred.

A person is programmed to move towards his genetic given, a body of a certain size and weight. Even when obstacles get in his way, he moves in that direction. A person may have his rightful body size, yet lack the attributes that go with it. He may look like an adult from the outside, but lack the internal feeling. As he recognizes this discrepancy, he may assume a compensatory shape to appear adult. To appear self-confident before his boss, he may stiffen himself in relation to his internal deficiency. Unboundedness or immaturity can also be a defense as well as a state of being. A person acts childlike to hide his intentions or to avoid the consequences. Shape always has both a social and a personal function. When assaulted or intimidated by another, a person responds with a shape to please, resist, fight back, or submit.

From a developmental perspective rigid, dense, swollen, and collapsed structures involve the relationship of the whole to the part. This means that, in a child, the upper part of the organism is more developed than the lower. As the child grows, the lower part develops. All the shapes of insult can be related to an imaginary dividing line, from birth to eight and from eight onward. This dividing line is based upon whether the structural emphasis is in the upper body or the lower body. From a developmental view, the question is at what point a person invests in the upper half of the body versus the lower half. Early growth and development is seen in the upper half of the organism, and after that time investment is in the lower half. Response patterns have to do with taking and responding, going to and from the world, and the pulsatory connection between the upper half of the body and the other person. Past age eight a person is more interested in maintaining his pulsatory connection to himself, not necessarily his connection to the other person. This is the foundation of autonomy and self-regulation.

Patterns of Distress / 12

Rigid

13 / Patterns of Distress

Dense

Patterns of Distress / 14

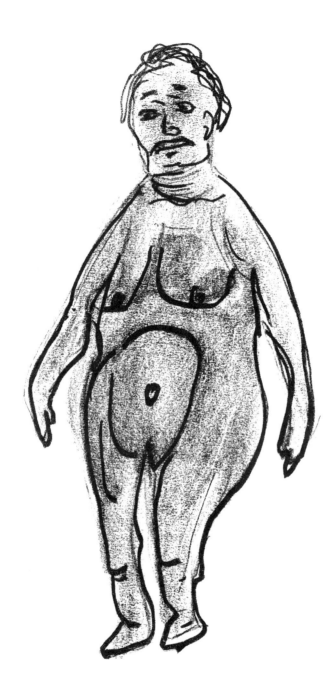

Swollen

15 / Patterns of Distress

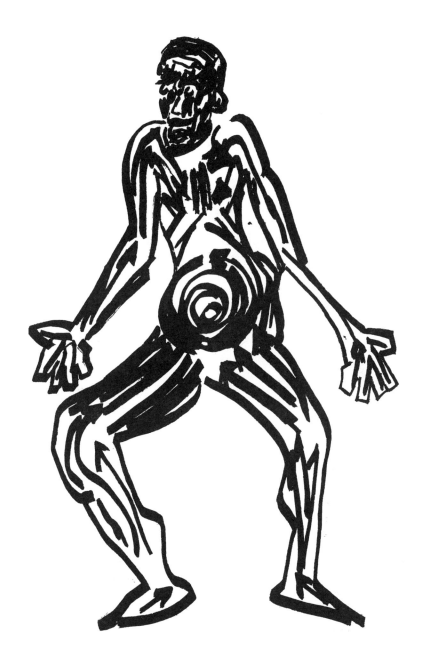

Collapsed

The Formative Concept

The foundation of human experience is the organization of the forms of a person's inheritance and the forms that express his experience. The clinical questions to ask are: What are the principles of this person's forming process and what is it that he is trying to form? This process represents the ground floor, the shape a person is able to organize and function as. The child is trying to work his way to adulthood. What does it mean to be a child? It means to have the form and shape of a child as he deals with his responses, learning to shape his relationship in the present on his way to tomorrow. Likewise an adult is on his way to maturity, a crystalization of his talents and individuality. Every new impulse to growth is experienced as having youthful qualities. If an adult rejects his earlier experiences of forming, he may reject other things which are new.

The formative concept implies that overbound and underbound shapes are statements of a personal history, but these shapes may not be a statement of the future. Because a client presents himself to a somatic therapist as an overbound shape, it does not mean that he will be that way forever. The formative principle introduces a revolutionary concept having to do with the way a person organizes or forms himself throughout his life.

Using the analogy of a flexible tube, overbound and underbound structures can be thought of as a rigid or spastic, dense, swollen, or collapsed. The loss of shape and the narrowing or thickening of boundaries give a therapist clues as to the nature of his client. Figure One points out that shock runs clear across the organism. A client can be shocked to death or congealed in such a way that liquids are no longer moving. By retreating into his center, the client keeps alive vegetatively but he may never recover. Alternatively, shock and trauma may affect segments of the organism. One part of the organism may be dense and thickened while another part is swollen.

Generally speaking, overbound clients try to maintain a semblance of independence; the swollen client maintains a facade of independence but seeks to ride piggyback on someone else. The weak and collapsed person has the shape of dependence and seeks the dependent response. He walks into a therapist's office asking for help and the therapist's first response is, "Here, let me help you." This repeats the client's experience in growing up. His structure should be understood as asking for shape not dependency.

Overbounded and underbounded are not only organismic states, they are states of personal existence. When a therapist deals with spasticity, brittleness, shock, or abuse, he has to ask himself how deep these states go, what is involved, what does one layer present compared to another layer, what is the general picture and what is the specific picture of the client, how much adult or childlike form is present? Is this person a spastic person or is his spasticity a superficial form protecting an unformed inner visceral layer?

One indication of somatic immaturity is how quickly the client can change his shape. A child is plastic, he can change shape instantaneously, he is relatively unbound on his way to becoming bound. When an adult has this ability, a therapist will recognize that his client has not organized much structure. This is not to say that a client cannot change his shape over a relatively short period of time, but his ability to do so and the time that this takes is related to the degree and layering of his underboundedness or overboundedness.

Maturity involves the ability to form a structure that represents one's experience and to live with it without becoming a victim to it. For example, it may be necessary for an overbound person to hold his ground in a particular situation; however, when that situation has passed, he should be able to relax it. This is a mark of maturity. How much change occurs, and over how great a span of time, indicates the nature of a client's unformedness.

The ability to change shape is what is significant. In a child, reflexes and involuntary responses bring about changes in shape. This is also true for a grownup. But an adult can participate in his changing shape. For example, a person may be outraged but choose not to express anger, to fight or to hurt another person's feelings. Therefore, he takes his whole organization of being enraged and modifies it volitionally. This is the difference between an impulsive person and a person who is capable of managing himself. The shape that a person has and how he organizes a shape for himself is a statement about being grownup or being a child.

The essence of the struggle of formativeness is self-management. In primitive societies, being at one with nature and being lived by nature are the highest goals. In our world we say, "go with the flow." To my mind, formativeness and self-management mean to use one's experiences to form an internal self that takes care of a multitude of needs—to feed and shelter one's self and to carry on social interactions of a particular kind that result in a personal subjective form. It takes work to form an internal self, it just doesn't happen. It does not help a client to perpetuate his philosophy of "just let it happen." Nothing just happens; a client has to use himself to organize behavior. In a child we call this practicing.

Patterns of Insult: Summing Up

In forming himself, a client runs across an obstacle. He mobilizes himself to deal with it. His first response is to challenge, to push against, to run away, to hit, or to go around it. His second response is to hold it off or to hold his ground so that he has another level of rigidity. Once he feels that a threat is getting to him and he can do nothing about it, he attempts placation, merges with the aggressor, and shows that he is not a threat. Finally, he disengages, gives up form, and collapses.

Shock leads to a frozen, spastic form. The result of the insult is overboundedness. Trauma evokes overactivity first, then gradually disintegration and underboundedness emerge. Abuse stunts form; it keeps it underformed and unstable. Neglect keeps a person from becoming formed. Insult, therefore, organizes shapes with too much or too little form.

Overbounded and underbounded are relative. These structure are responses to an event or a condition. A young person is relatively unbounded on his way to increasing organization and complexity, overcoming youthful unformedness. Solidification of shape occurs between underbounded and overbounded, where a middle ground, a combination expresses the organism and forms an image of its inside.

Insults refer to structural breakdowns, obstacles which produce organizational discrepancies. Overbound and underbound structures are not absolutes but are related to specific situations. A therapist can never say that nature meant a client to be underbound unless nature made a mistake. Rather, something has happened that broke down the client's formative process. The question is how the client will restore his boundaries. While I talk about insults in polarized terms, I am not talking about the relationship of one pole to the other, but about a process that incorporates both poles—a relativistic situation.

Some responses to insult are more functional than others. The least functional stages are in the center of Figure One. Shock can be mild or severe, but it always immobilizes the individual. A person is least functional at this point. Trauma, at the outset, demands action but it then immobilizes the person. Abuse is more functional than abandonment. At an early age, abandonment or neglect produces shock; at a later age it is only moderately dysfunctional. Abuse cripples a person and limits him to low-level functioning.

Sydney: The Crushed Child

Sydney is a man with a form that is spoon-like, concave in front with a body like a bent handle. His head is out in front of his body. He is pulled in, compacted, and collapsed. Sydney is cognitively aggressive yet experiences episodes of volcanic outburst. He seeks love yet his ambition demands he succeed and win. While he is quite successful in the world, he feels incompetent.

Sydney's form resulted from a long, repetitious pattern of insult that affected his self-esteem. Although he was cared for as a child and adolescent, he was also subjected to demands that he be more than he was. He was supposed to live up to someone else's standards. In the face of this onslaught he compacted himself, retreated, surrendered his ground, and collapsed inward. In order to cover his weakness, he constructed an outer form of aggression and striving. Sydney is small attempting to be big, beaten down but resisting collapse.

Sydney describes his background:
My parents attempted to shape my growth and personality through guilt. They did not intentionally set out to do this, but they set goals I could not meet or, when I did meet them, remarked that I had fallen short. This pattern occurred from as early as I can remember until age eighteen when I broke off all relations with my parents for a year to establish my own independence. The sense of guilt causes confusion for me. On the one hand, it appears to have been major and constant, on the other hand, perhaps it was mild and moderate but appeared different to the fragile child that I was.

The main attitude I adopted was dissociation but my secondary attitudes included fight, helplessness, hopelessness, manic frenzy, and disorientation. At an early age, I experienced disbelief and thought that my real parents were locked away in the basement while the parents I experienced were unkind marauders who had robbed me of my true benevolent parents. By age seven or eight that disbelief faded and I accepted my reality. These were my parents and this was to be my life.

Now I realize that the reason for their constant criticism was that I was not the boy my parents needed. From my mother I developed a sense of insecurity because she indicated that my needs were bad. This constant state of being cared for while rejected and criticized confused me. My parents became a source of pain, irritation, annoyance. I felt guilty and angry, small and helpless.

The effect on me now that I am grown is that I find myself on automatic pilot as a performer and struggler. I keep myself so busy being a struggler that I tend to be out of contact with myself as well as with others and this pattern tends to perpetuate itself. The more I work with myself somatically, the more I am able to re-establish self-contact and experience my own rhythms. My constant struggle to avoid disappointing the universe lessens. My struggle not to disappoint is pervasive and requires constant vigilance and a great deal of love and outside help to overcome. The struggling represents my

Patterns of Distress / 20

Sydney
Defeat on the outside, defiance on the inside

Sydney's form represents a rigid/weak structure, an insult pattern based upon constant parental criticism, discouragement and intimidation. The result is humiliation.

Sydney is collapsed, his chest is pulled in, his diaphragm is flattened and descended, his abdomen has poor tone, his esophagus and trachea are elongated and constricted.

attempt to prevent my form from breaking down. It is a conflict between submission and aggression, collapse and attack. It is an overwhelming and wonderful experience when my inner self overcomes my parentally conditioned attitude.

At any given time, if I do not dominate the "struggle to not disappoint" attitude, it begins to dominate me. What astounds me is how wonderfully real, contactful, and satisfying my life is when I overcome this attitude and the good in me emerges. Contrary to my everyday belief, my efficiency increases when I take time out to work on myself. Unfortunately, however, this requires a structure that I normally do not create.

I do not remember a time when this attitude did not exist, although it was only in later life that I discovered the love-starved child within me. Earlier on my self-image was one of hiding, not wanting to be noticed, not wanting others to see how needy I was. In practicing somatic exercise, my subjective experience is that my body has been attacked from all fronts. I experience myself pulling in and hiding, while at the same time I dissociate in an attempt not to lose the fight. I experience this as an immediate and intense contraction in my entire abdomen. When I disorganize this stance, I experience a gentle move towards expansion and an accompanying feeling of relaxation. I also experience two inner images of myself: a stunted, shrunken me with feelings of inferiority, which I live with all the time, and, on more and more occasions, a filled-out, bigger bodied me who feels more generous and manly.

The accordion exercise of doing it more and doing it less is most useful to me. It provides a starting point which is simple to remember. I am able to control the emotional, physical, and intellectual panic I experience when I feel inadequate to perform a task. During the pause, I experience a state somewhat between relief and resignation, humility and collapse, relaxation and self-acceptance. I experience clarity when I work with my therapist or during a workshop with him. When I am by myself, I often experience my process as confusing. I find that I need another's response to offset the unspoken philosophy of my father to do it alone.

Clinical Comment: In my work with Sydney I had him organize, his pattern of shrinking in his chest and shoulders over and over again in order to mobilize the feelings of criticism and abuse. As he was able to disorganize his structure, I was able to help him integrate the tender pulsations in his chest and his feelings of longing, rejection, and fear. As Sydney disorganized his shrinking, self-assertive feelings arose in his thorax and a new self-esteem emerged. The next step was to develop specific practices for Syndey to engage in at work and in his marriage to give solidity to his new form. Working to form himself in the presence of others was central to the type of insult that Sydney experienced.

Sharon: An Encounter with Mortality

Sharon is a powerful woman whose posture represents self-affirmation and territorial possession. She can also be rigid, unyielding, and self-righteous. Her appearance is like a top sergeant's—chest up, stomach flat, neck stiff, at attention.

Recently, Sharon was involved in an accident that affected her social and personal self. Her injuries exaggerated her existing pulled-up pattern and alienated her even more from her instinctual self. Her adult form and ongoing identity were interfered with as she came face-to-face with her own mortality.

Sharon describes her accident as follows:
About three years ago, after returning home from having dinner with friends, I parked my car outside of my home. As I got out of the car and locked the door, I saw a car rapidly coming towards me on the street. Without warning, the car struck me and threw me against the windshield and onto the pavement. At that moment, the situation took on the timelessness and slow-motion effect of a dream, all action was incredibly slowed down. I was numb but aware of what was going on around me. I noticed that the car sped off, and that the street was deserted. I remembered my neighbor who often sat at his window; I feared that I might pass out. At the same time I had a sense of disbelief and an awareness that this should not be happening to me.

I raised my head and screamed with all my might, hoping that my neighbor would hear me. I screamed more for anyone who might give me assistance. As I did so I felt something wet on my face, realized it was blood, and that I had been badly injured. I tried to stagger to my feet, but fell to the ground still calling out for help. When my neighbors came out to me, I began issuing directions: "Stop the flow of blood, get me a blanket, call the police." Finally the police arrived, and I was taken to the hospital in an ambulance with its siren screaming. I dimly recall that this worried me even more.

The preceding events took no more than a few minutes but were followed by hours of tests at the hospital as the doctors tried to discover whether I had a concussion or spinal injuries. Finally, I had to be anesthetized in order for the doctors to stitch my head up. My emotional states included surprise, determination to save myself, and

23 / *Patterns of Distress*

Sharon
Surprise, Shock, Disbelief, Challenge, Defiance

Sharon is inflated, assertive, and rejecting. Her goal is to ward off or to keep others away. Sharon's chest is pulled-up and arched, her buttocks, thighs, spine and neck are stiff, her abdomen is taut and protruding.

finally, a dreamlike sense of unreality that such bizarre events could happen to me so suddenly. In retrospect I realize that my response to the accident occurred in differing stages: at first I experienced disbelief and organized myself as if to attack; then I became aware of the shock of the hit and run and the panic at being alone, next I felt pain as I was in the ambulance and hospital, and finally fear and the feelings of helplessness overcame me.

Even today, several years after the hit and run, this accident affects my life. I am prone to imagine bad things happening to me if I go out walking on the street or driving. I have to stop myself from daydreaming that I might be in an accident again. I become fearful when I see cars going fast or drivers racing their engines while waiting for the stoplights to change. I am even more afraid if these events occur when it is dark. I am so fearful that I often ask friends to drive me somewhere at night and I am inclined to get home early. While these extreme fears are fading, occasionally something in the environment reminds me of that night and triggers the same feelings of fear.

The physical stance I assume in response to the insult is to stiffen and brace like I was readying myself to fight or run. I experience this primarily in my back, neck, calves, and upper arms. My realization that control can be taken away from me occasionally deepens into panic and obsessive thoughts. Will I be out of control again? If so, how can I get back in control of myself or the situation? These fears are accompanied by a feeling of hopelessness and a deadly sense of despair which I try to overcome by doing something active or calling a friend. I find myself seeking more contact with others than I had in the past so that I am not alone as much, something I quite enjoyed before my accident. I experience myself being more alert, watchful, and wary when I am in public. It is at these moments that I experience the bracing again.

My subjective experience of that event was of something totally unexpected happening outside of my control. I did not feel victimized at the time, but later as the glow of support from family and friends wore off, I had to fight my fears in order to function. I first experienced fear, then anger. It was another shock for me to realize that I was never totally in control of my life, a belief I had previously held. I had to organize myself to be cautious and careful and hold my breath. Before my accident, I had an inner image of powerfulness and extroversion, now I experience myself as brittle, shrinking, and pulling away. I have lost my spirit of adventure and fearlessness.

Experiencing how I organize my body and emotional responses gives me a sense of again being in charge of myself. When an old stimulus sets off fear, I can identify the stiffening and bracing.

Either I can throw off the fear by softening my body stance, or, if and when it is too much for me, I can change my environment. Though no external scars remain, the insult is marked forever in me and would control my life were I not able to identify and reorganize some of its somatic pattern.

The accordion exercise of expansion and contraction is useful to me. When I exaggerate my stance, I find it easier to identify the separate bodily components of my stress pattern. My consciousness increases as does my control of the different aspects of the pattern. I am able to reorganize another feeling. This exercise teaches me self-control and self-management by demonstrating that my emotional states are something I have some influence over. This attitude is more satisfying than endlessly trying to control the world and other people in it. Now I can stop the process of bracing and obsessing by exaggerating and releasing the stress pattern. I realize there is a way to relate to my dreaded emotions, fear and despair, differently. They will not be endless nor can they control my life without my acquiesence.

The pattern I used to brace for the impact of the auto was an exaggeration of how I organize my ongoing defense, the spastic bracing that forms my bravado. When this disorganizes, I feel the terror of the unexpected. As I learn how to disorganize the fear pattern, I discover that self-management is different than obsessively controlling.

In disorganizing the bracing of trauma and my fear, my vulnerability became more acceptable. Deep feelings of gentleness and a delightful inner stream of pleasureable excitation began to occur. I can, in fact, let down my bravado to this inner self. As I learn to settle into this safe vulnerability, I realize that I had not only changed my body shape but also my set of values. My accident has become my teacher; the patterns of shock and trauma have organized a new sense of self, a more receptive personal self.

Somatic-Emotional Breakdown

Feeling is generated not only through movement. The shape that a person has organized represents the way he feels about himself. This understanding is at the ground floor of somatic work.

As a person's cellular, tissue, and organ motility change, so do his feelings and thoughts about himself. He organizes a different somatic image and possible self. If a man's ego ideal or social role demand he maintain his youthful masculinity or strength, he will be in conflict between an organismic attempt to reorganize and his ego's need to maintain present form. This conflict is not merely psychological or emotional. It is a structural conflict, a conflict of body shapes.

It is said that a therapist should offer support to a client. But what does support mean? It is the recognition of how the client organizes a form for himself. To be supportive means to assist the client to disorganize what is inappropriate and organize more appropriately according to the client's own rules. Support does not mean holding the client's hand or withholding criticism. It means helping a client form his own ideas or action and learning from his own experience. The client's feeling of competence then rests upon his ability to manage what arises for him. He may not be able to manage the outside world, but he can manage himself.

Pulsation—the Core of the Organizing Process

Fundamental to the organizing process is a phenomena I call pulsation, a unique and archetypal movement. Pulsation is a pristine and profound pattern that organizes and funnels excitation along a pathway to create a shape. Heartbeat is a pulsation with which everyone is familiar. If it were viewed on a sonargram, one would see an echo series of schematic images, somewhat like on a radar screen, of the heart's movements over time. The heart expands and contracts in a particular shape under different conditions over time. That enduring morphology shapes itself according to the challenges that it meets; sometimes there is an increase in movement, sometimes a decrease. When that pulsatory shape is interfered with, there is a complete change in the consciousness and the responsiveness of a person.

The fundamental pulsatory pattern, in-and-out, forms a perimeter, a surface, and an interior. The extremes of its movements represent a pattern that has an outer and an inner boundary. The rhythm and amplitude of the heart's movement sets up a series of membranes and structures that maintain a living morphology over time. The person's movement, perception, thinking and emotions all represent this. Each and every person is a pulsating pattern of great complexity.

Pulsation is a dynamic force which must be maintained in order to have an identity or a certain life expression. It gives rise to the sensations that create the primitive body image. This pulsatory pattern is billions of years old and is the ancient wisdom of every person. Its movement captures the recorded experience of all of creation up until now and makes it available for the entire organism to knows its history, its embodiment, and its shape. Somatic reality is this deep, embedded in pulsatory patterns.

To those who can read it, the pulsatory pattern is reflected in the dreams and images which people have, no matter how covered over by the social images one uses to describe his external reality. If a person permits himself, he can feel it in breathing, in standing, in being quiet, in how he moves. He recognizes a surface, an outside, he recognizes an inside, a place of deeper intensity or repose, and he recognizes a middle. Who is it that recognizes these dimensions? The pattern recognizes itself, since the pulsation moving through a continuum of spaces sets up the sensations and feelings that act as a dialogue between one level and the other. It talks to itself. Then an individual describes it as something that is distant from or separate from himself: "I experience my body." It is, in fact, the level of pulsation, as it spreads or slows through a continuum of levels of its own pattern, that sets up self-dialogue or self-knowing. The dialogue is in the layers of sensation in the cross-section of movement. One does not have to assume a separate, independent entity that is somehow directing the show. The show is directed by itself, by this movement which is at the very ground floor of all existence.

The function of the organizing process is to maintain this pulsatory rhythm in response to a shape that is being organized. When the pulsatory pattern finds resistance to its outward movement, to its assertive thrust into the world, it will stiffen or speed itself up in an attempt to overwhelm the irritant. Alternately, it will shrink from the surface in an attempt to hibernate or wait out the irritant. A clinician recognizes these patterns in clients who are rigid or collapsed, manic or depressive, fighting or engaging in passive resistance.

When a clinician pays attention to how a client pulsates or how his pulsation is organized on a higher level of expression, he is struck by a major fact: a person is a process rooted in an environment, a matrix that includes others as well as himself. There is a movement, a form by which one is with his environment, with others, and with himself. This movement goes on simultaneously—part of it may be in the foreground, part in the background. A person may be more alert to that part which is himself rather than his background, but he has a background. The shape that he maintains, his moving shape, is similar to a three-legged stool made up of a planetary environment, a social environment, and his personal shape. The connection to this three legged environment is what somatic sanity is, the feeling and the experience of being rooted in something bigger than one's self.

When this pulsating pattern meets severe restrictions or is ignored in one sphere or another, a person finds himself rootless, ungrounded, without a history. He hopes desperately for a future of connection. This describes our present culture. We are caught up in a localized, specialized pulsation in our heads, temporarily moving it to our genitals yet totally unconnected to its overt feeling and its history of developement as well as our relation to others. Our frightened, isolated self's hope is that tomorrow will be better, yet we do not know how to form such a tomorrow.

Physical Reorganization—The Key

Every challenge of sufficient proportion gets the organism's attention and brings about a change in inner shape. This urge to reform one's shape can become chronic, sub-acute, or acute. It follows a specific pattern along the pathway of frustration, trauma, or shock. Shock can accompany inner and outer transitional stages of one's life. These changes are accompanied by reorganization, a change in emotional shape, which is not always appreciated.

The first three pictures of Figure One demonstrate the progression of the startle response: pay attention, investigate, surprise. These stances, ranging from surprise to real alarm, reflect how one is in the world. A deer who grazes in a field is simply in the world. If something catches its attention, the first organization stops and the animal immediately braces and pays attention. The deer reorganizes.

Present-day culture places an enormous value on being attentive, the first stance. The attentive posture is assumed to be normal and natural, and carries an accompanying reward system: a person who pays attention is good, one who does not is bad. The first of the three positions on the startle continuum means, attentiveness, what is this, should I pay attention; next, fear and attack, an intensification of stiffening; and last, turning away, a further intensification into the flight pattern.

All three postures involve a shift in shape. A young child, for example, may respond to abuse with fear. As he enters adolescence, he maintains a stiff pattern which he now experiences as his normal posture. The startle continuum illustrates that insults involve changes in shape, a stiffening of the organism, an ascent upwards, and shifts in the entire organism.

Changes in shape imply changes in activity. The first three images show overboundedness—an increase in form, organization, structure, and activity. This increase in activity is not necessarily physical movement, but may be felt as excitation or anxiety.

The crossover line between an increase and a decrease in form occurs in the third position. As the increase in structure becomes oppressive, the organism responds with inhibition and depression. If the insult continues, helplessness, submission, hopelessness, and apathy arise. Finally, a person retreats into collapse.

Overbound and underbound structures are either overactive or underactive, overformed or underformed. The startle image dramatizes the relationship between the body wall and the visceral spaces, the surfaces and the interior, and how the organism may compartmentalize itself. Deformity occurs in one of two ways, through diminution or enlargement. The organs in the chest wall or the abdomen receive either too much or too little pressure.

The first half of the startle sequence show images which inflate and become bigger, while the latter half represent images which become smaller and deflate. These are the two different defenses: bluff and puff or withdrawal and shrinking. A person goes from overactivity, convulsion, hysteria and mania to underactivity, hibernation, coma, apathy, and listlessnness.

Collapse, the end of the startle continuum, is an organization. It may be a poor organization but it is a structure. A therapist, in dealing with this type of structure, must first understand how a client organizes his collapse. For example, collapse involves a reflex pattern of giving-up. This represents an organization that guarantees the collapse, the hibernation of the oxygenating mechanism, since collapse and deoxygenation go together. On one level, a client may disorganize his inhibiting mechanisms rather than increase his breathing. The therapist should begin to destructure what is overstructured. Alternately, the therapist could increase the visceral motility in the collapsed area, building a sense of pulsation and generating organ motility, excitation, and feeling. Another way would be for the therapist to use his communication with the client as a catalyst.

Action is organized in a layered pattern. There is a genetic, neural, emotional blueprint to action. To get ready to act a person invokes a set of muscular patterns and then increases these patterns in order to act. A person goes from enervating his muscle-spindle group, organizing the minimal amount that represent his action until he organizes the whole muscle action pattern. Three levels are involved—upper brain, midbrain, brainstem. The outside of a person is his habitual attitude, his action in process. If he goes back one step, he finds the action that is preparing to be acted on. If he goes back one step more into the central nervous system, he has the attitude as a pattern that has not been activated muscularly.

Recently, a male client told me that after his marriage was over he could not find another relationship. As he talked to me, I pointed out how he was presenting himself with a focused intensity. When I encouraged him to increase his intensity, a suspicious stance emerged as if to ask, "What do you want from me?" His focusing was an attempt to keep other people at a distance and then try to get something from them.

When my client was thirteen his father died and his mother was left with three children to support. I connected this critical event to his present physical stance and his presenting complaint. I discovered that he could talk to men but not to women. He said that he had trouble with people because he is always looking for the devil or what is wrong with them. He explained, "I do not want to get involved with someone because then I might not be able to get out. I look for the devil in others to maintain my own distance and hide my own need to be dependent." I noted his physical stance, pulled up, braced for attack, neck, eyes, chest, stomach, and legs rigid as if he were scared, overly suspicious, and distrustful. This lived pattern resulted in his isolation.

We began a somatic dialogue, using language and feeling to connect his past emotional experience to his present somatic organization of extreme focusing and suspicion. My current goal for this client is to help him begin to make simple demands around a few basic needs. I am not trying to take away his stiffness, something that may happen five years from now. Rather, I am trying to build a structure for communication. By teaching my client to disorganize, I am taking him down a layer somatically as well as historically. I encourage him to stay in his pushing-away attitude so that he will have some support.

Body Image

A person has one body image made up of a natural, societal, and a personal layer. The basic body image organizes where everything is in relation to the space around a person and his internal space. On the first level, the image involves connective tissue (ligaments, bone, striated muscle, the spindle level) and spatial orientation (being upright, walking, movement). The second level relates body image to the emotional situation that a person is embedded in and his need. For example, "I want closeness, when I am big I do not get it, when I am small I do." Then there is a sociological level, "This is how I want others to see me." These three levels make up one's body image. There is a fourth one, the basic constitutional given.

One of the functions of process is to organize an external and internal logic and to organize into non-pictoral and then pictoral patterns of inner and outer experience. The image is a circuit, a geometric pattern converted into objects that the society teaches so the organism can talk to itself. By introjecting the culturally identified objects, one can make social sense out of his internal sense.

The men who received the Nobel prize for their work on vision established that the occipital lobe builds up a series of images which it converts into a social order, step by step. A person does not perceive the world as it is directly; he makes the world visually in the occipital lobe of his brain. As the world is processed through each layer, all those occipital cells are geometrically arranged in shape. There is a different layering at each of those levels. Body image, then, is a buildup of layers of experience into shapes that talk to each other to influence behavior.

Splitting

There is an urge to form in the organism. A child is programmed to grow up, to become an adult. I do not mean "grown up" in its sociological definition but in its organismic shape, function, and action, a biological definition. When an organism experiences something from inside or outside itself that it is not prepared to deal with, its defensive response may interrupt this pattern of growth. A child's brain cannot make sense of too much stimulation or inappropriate excitation. The unexpected upwelling of uncontrollable impulses causes fear and pain.

There is a structured series of responses to an obstacle; frustration, confusion, helplessness, the beginning of disorientation, indecision, and, finally, self-alienation. When a person cannot organize himself to deal with a problem, he sacrifices more and more parts of himself. He keeps one part of himself alive and splits off or sacrifices other functions. This process is painful because a person's organismic wholeness as well as his psychological self is wounded and inflamed.

Splitting involves an organismic state of dislike, "I have to get away from this," "Should I attack or should I run?" The organism is

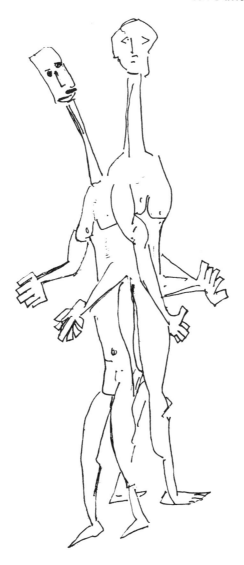

Splitting
*Twisting and Turning, Ambivalence and Avoidance
Dissociation and Compartmentalization*

A twofold pattern, to escape yet stay put: one part runs away and the other focuses and faces forward.

This pattern involves denial and conflict from which one cannot escape. Two separate self-identities result, the coward and the hero, the doer and the doubter. One part can be rigid and dense, the other small and weak.

caught between pushing away, ejecting, and avoiding. There is confusion and indecision. The organism is capable of making a separation or compartmentalization between its cognitive function and its feeling. This split involves two motor, muscular action patterns, to stay and to run. One part of the organism—an organ function, a feeling, a sensation—freezes as if it were an enemy or something to be kept away from. Muscular action patterns are mobilized to keep the "enemy" sequestered.

A person's emotional stance is always going on and forms the basis for his thinking and action. In splitting, a person is unaware of part of himself. At some level he says, "I split this off from my experience." Does that mean that it is no longer there? If a client enters into somatic work, he experiences this split. This organismic readiness to go in two directions, two separate muscular actions, sets up a perceived ambivalence and a sense of "being torn apart."

Splitting has clinical implications. A sense of self-reference, not regressive material, shows up as a client reforms himself. As a client recalls an event, the therapist may think that he is reliving past experience. In fact, recollection may be the only reference the client has to describe a state he is now in while he is on the way to his next state. Confusion arises if a therapist believes that the discovery of a historical state reconstitutes the client. Rather, the historical state is a part of somatic reorganization. These are completely different events. A therapist is not dealing solely with regressive material.

It is frightening for a client to be unsure of his state. He cannot orient himself. If the client is overwhelmed with anxiety, he will search his memory bank for another time he experienced similar feelings. In establishing a reference point, somatic organization comes into play. One recollects not only the event but the physicality of the event registered as motor memory. When a therapist destructures a client, he must deal with the physicality of the memory, not only the "insight" it provides.

On the Way to the Self

A person senses that his own way of doing something is right. Any interference with this self-affirming urge calls out a particular reaction. There is an increase in activity accompanied by a determination that says, "My way is right."(Chart One) The forward-going movement of the organism is interrupted. This increased activity—anger or fear—splits the person from his ongoing movement and begins a descent which may end up in hopelessness, helplessness, or despair.

35 / *Patterns of Distress*

Integrity / Obstacle	Compensation	Organization	Feelings
→	Anger	Overbound (increased organization)	Mania Hysteria Rejection Inflation
→	Fear		
→	Helplessness	Wait	Floundering Uselessness Inevitability
→	Hopelessness	Underbound (decreased organization)	Withdrawal Depression
→	Despair		

CHART ONE: On the Way to the Self

When the integrity of the self is challenged, a person compensates with a series of responses to preserve and maintain himself.

A person's belief system grows out of his organization. Each place along the descent has its own rationalization and carries its own fear because of what the person has left and what may be ahead. A fearful person is afraid of his own anger (one step upward) as well as helplessness (one step downward). He rationalizes that the meek shall inherit the earth. Another person who is angry may believe that others are out to get him, therefore he will attack first.

On the way to forming maturity, challenges and insults produce feelings of self-affirmation followed by aggressive compensation. "Damn it, I am right," is the verbal statement. Self-righteousness and rationalizations emerge and head toward the obstacle. If the insult is powerful or if one is constitutionally disposed, a person may decide to investigate it before he attacks. If the obstacle scares him, he may not know what to do. If he is overwhelmed, he may lay down and let the obstacle roll over him. He may make himself as big as possible and attack, organize himself to wait, or make himself as small as possible in hopes that the obstacle goes away. These are the different startle stances.

When a person decides his best strategy is to wait, he shifts from increased to decreased organization. As he deflects from meeting the obstacle head on, he begins to split or separate from his goal. In saving the basic self, a person preserves one set of attitudes while he organizes a different set. He compartmentalizes himself.

There is order in the organism. Order is experienced, first, as pulsation, a reliable, continuous experience of self-recognition such as breathing or the heartbeat. This pulsation gives a basic sense of order from which a person can discover his own inner order or consciously how to make order. Structure is function. There cannot be a function without a structure, there cannot be a structure without a function. Structure has organization, just as function does. There is an inner order to sustaining a form, and to disorganizing behavior. A person under stress goes through bounding and unbounding in order to maintain or give up form. The experience of forming and unforming is an experience of order.

Mania can accompany fear and anger. The minute a person runs into an obstacle, he increases his motility and excitation which can begin a manic cycle, an unbounded increase in excitation, pulsation, and activity to resolve an issue. Mania is closely linked to panic and hysteria. Mania is an overactive, out-of-control state of increased disorganization. The manic person feels driven to maintain order and form by chasing his tail. He is trying to preserve whatever structure he has and to prevent it from collapsing. He is not trying to get rid of energy but to avoid failure. In the social realm, mania becomes hysteria, aggression, or attack.

Increase and decrease in organization shows up with a client. For example, when I get a client to increase motility and excitation, I find that his insight, perception, and sensation increase. If the excitation is unrestricted, it turns into mania and unboundedness. At that point, I ask the client how he talks obsessively or how he can use his own self-management to inhibit his over-activity.

Many people do not recognize the sequence involved in the behavior that causes them problems. A client may recognize he is getting more depressed, but he may not know the sequence of steps so he cannot interfere with it. In the therapeutic situation, if a client is taught how he responds to obstacles, he has a chance to deal with them in a way that is not too complicated. I have a patient who has mild epileptic attacks. We talk about his disorganization process. Part of it is the loss of binocular vision as his head twists; it is the beginning of convulsive behavior. When he feels an attack coming on, he is able to shortcut it by disorganizing the averting reflex in the neck. This may not always solve an incipient epileptic attack but he can learn to interfere with the disorganizing process.

Once a client recognizes what his pattern is, he can interfere with it. He may be fearful, but it is better than helplessness. Then he can attack the fear pattern. It is not only a question of what makes a person helpless, but how he disorganizes his response to helplessness. Fear does not have to lead to terror. A client can disorganize his terror and live with a little fear. From fear he can return to a mild degree of annoyance rather than going from fear to comfort. This model for somatic therapy recognizes that the brain acts along a sequential and ordered pathway.

As an individual builds a personal body, he organizes an interior life. For me, an internal life is not the images that reflect the process, but the experiences of the process organizing an interior shape. It is different than the roles that a person plays. A person is the organizer of his experience. The personal body is the actual source of an inner shape. It is not just a mental state. It requires an inner pattern of pulsation, a feeling state, and an internal conversation between personal associations, memories, and present actions that reflect the basic cellular or tissue state. Then an original brain circuit is evoked which helps smooth and striated muscles to make an internal and external somatic form.

An increase in activity challenges a person's self-control. It begins self-affirming behavior which can lead to anger, compartmentalization, or avoidance. The social personality is still maintained. As his attempts to ward off the insult fail, he descends and enters the low brain and becomes an instinctual creature.

An overactive, overexcitable, impulsive person is extra alert and thinks his paranoia is an intelligence. A person who is inflated and puffed-up swims in his own images without any organization. These are two entirely different states. The manic person does not bluff, he believes his projections. The swollen person is all bluff; he exaggerates and deceives. Withdrawal and depression are reflex responses and are in a category of their own.

Both overbound and underbound structures put big demands upon a therapist and call for different responses. The therapist has to provide structure for an overactive as well as an unbounded person. With the unbounded and collapsed, he has to intervene because the client melts into nothingness. The kind of bonding such a client wants indicates where to intervene. The unbounded wants a relationship in which the therapist contains him, so he makes the therapist think he is like him. An inflated person may organize a relationship with his therapist where he is allowed to be big. These are quite different. What is the shape that the client shows a therapist? A nice, well-organized client may tell a therapist that he is a little angry, but a distressed person may present himself in a more disorganized way. A client's shape indicates how a therapist should relate. For example, I have a male client who is sociable, well-ordered, rigid, compulsive, polite, a follower of the rules. His behavior masks a frenzied form of male panic and overactivity. He wants me to keep my distance yet soothe his panic. The challenge is how to organize his panic, how to form excitement from formlessness, how to turn overstimulation into feeling and behavior.

Once a client realizes that life is an unending challenge either to maintain or to form his life he can make a choice. He can take the attitude of the autonomic nervous system and engage in a comfortable dialogue with the vegetative function as it swings from pleasure to stress. Or he may identify with the central nervous system which is always concerned with social performance. He may choose some place in the middle. How he organizes his life depends on knowing certain steps. How does a person maintain his form? How does he participate in the transformative parts of life? How does he form his life? These are the basic questions.

How a person uses himself is the key to his life. This is what a therapist has to teach a client—how he uses himself—his voice, his thought, his action, his feeling. Overbounded and underbounded shapes represent a misuse of one's self and force the individual to revert to automatic mechanisms. The further down the scale of the startle stances one goes, the less personal he is. He has surrendered a personal interaction with the world for a reflex action.

Insults from Internal Sources

Every person has three selves—the instinctual self, the social self, and the personal self. The instinctual self is the way of nature or the prepersonal; the social self refers to the rules and rituals of society, the postpersonal; and the personal self is what the individual has and must construct for himself. A personal self is not given at birth. When one becomes an adult it is possible for a personal self to develop. The natural self is given by the genetic code, the societal self develops through social upbringing. A personal self is the difference between acting according to the rules of society or one's own instinct's and doing things one's own way. These are important differences. Each person as a formative process must do things his own way yet he must also obey the laws of nature and society.

Insults do not come solely from parental or societal sources. An insult can come from inside as well as from outside a person. Different layers of a person can terrorize other layers. Hungers and instincts can be in conflict with his personal self, or social and economic needs can conflict with instinctual urges. All three selves are merged into one and also can be insulted through their relationship to one another. A conflict may be between nature and individual desire as in the case of a student who prepares for an exam until he is so exhausted that he cannot perform well. It may be a conflict between a person's own nature and how he has introjected society, someone who wishes to be artistic but who has been pressured to become a professional. Such dilemmas cause enormous internal struggle and are responsible for the peculiar shape every person has.

A former client once described in detail the raw, aggressive, and primitive feelings which welled up in her abdomen. These feelings threatened her in a way she had difficulty identifying. She became terrified of a force that might take her over. She feared she would disappear into a morass of wild and frenzied behavior. Her insult came from inside, the conflict between her own image as a proper, polite woman and her raw feelings of aggression. She felt her self-control and self-restraint system was in danger. Her insult was an internal upper body response to a visceral drive for survival located in the lower half. One part of herself was reacting to another part. Her form was breaking down because an upwelling of excitation was moving her towards an aggressive posture which threatened an equal urge to maintain her self-identity, a conflict between a prepersonal form and a postpersonal form. At the same time her personal self criticized the other two, the rising anger and the need to control it. This ongoing self-criticism became another level of insult. This had the effect of turning a very talented artist who had keen perceptions into a fearful person who panicked at her own vitality.

Kevin: The Shock of the Unexpected

Kevin is a tall mesomorph, a square, strong, action-oriented person, somewhat like a Viking, bold and expressive. He has a rigid, overbound stance. His life is adventurous and full of heroic exploits. While his appearance and action are bold, his feelings and subjective self are constricted, held back, reserved. He was brought up to perform for others and neglected his personal self.

Kevin was in an automobile accident, an intense and immediate trauma which was accompanied by a short period of shock. Kevin's accident reinforced a long history of needing to be a hero, braced and overactive. After the accident, Kevin was concerned as to why he did not perform better even though he was in a situation over which he had no control.

Kevin's insult pulled him up even more into his pattern of rigidity. It also served as the impetus for disorganizing his tendency to self-abuse, and to question his role as a performer. He had the opportunity to form a personal self that was not abusive and a social self that recognized others.

Kevin describes his accident:

About a year ago I ran into another car at fifty-five miles per hour as it pulled out from a blind intersection onto the main highway I was traveling. There was no way I could avoid the collision, even though I applied the brakes and swerved to the left. My wife, Sally, was sitting next to me at the time. In a short space of time, perhaps a few seconds, I watched the impact in seemingly slow motion and the subsequent crumpling, like a piece of paper, of the front end of my car. I was injured, although not in a major or permanently incapacitating way. I was psychologically traumatized. My self-esteem based upon performance and always being in control crumbled.

It seemed like I was in slow motion so that each second and miniscule event was sharply etched in my mind and body. My dominant attitude was disbelief until I realized I was not going to be able to avoid the collision; my attitude then changed as I could not take charge of the situation. My can-do attitude had been insulted. I was in shock, frozen. I was overcome by a sense of helplessness, more than I had ever known before.

This accident has had lasting effects upon me. Even now, a year later, I find that my muscles will tense up when I am driving. For

41 / Patterns of Distress

Kevin
Shock and Pain

Kevin's structure is rigid and combative. He is alert and prepared for attack or fight. This pattern results from demands for performance and emotional manipulation.

quite some months after the accident, I was mildly constipated, a condition I had not experienced before in my life. Since the collision, I have had almost a continuous series of chest colds and bronchitis verging on pneumonia due to the after effects of the severe bruising my chest took. Prior to the accident I led a physically active life. I now find I am not able to maintain that same level of energy. I no longer have the desire to carry on as I did before. Immediately after the wreck, I was nervous, jumpy, angry, and emotionally exhausted. I felt extremely sad about the injury my wife had sustained. I experienced myself crying as I drove to the hospital to visit her daily. I felt helpless to do anything about her situation.

With these emotional responses, I found myself full of self-doubt. I had a sense of floundering, I did not know what to do. I was in a crisis of values and action about my life in the world. Even today, I can recall in a total flashback of minute detail what happened in the collision. It is almost like watching a movie. This can occur at any time and serves to remind me that my world has changed. The state of helplessness returns. I experience contractions in my arms and face as if I want to thrash. Thankfully, I know how to undo this. When I do, I sense relief and feel, once again, that I have survived.

The collision as well as the somatic work I have done on myself, has challenged the linear model of thinking to which I had become accustomed. Now, in discussions with my wife or others, I am much more careful to listen, to consider choices, to pause and let things sink in before I respond with my "can-do" attitude. My thinking no longer has to be "right." I no longer try to force an idea out, but attempt to let it come out in its own time. However, I still experience my physical stance as alert, braced, pulled-up, somewhat ready to respond to outside danger. This is accompanied by the thoughts that I have "to watch out" or that the world is not quite as well organized as I presumed. The collision taught me that I am not always able to control what is happening to me. I may not always be able to perform as expected. As I begin to accept this truth, I find myself more accepting of others and less demanding of myself. I give myself more time to do things, and am content to do my best. As a consequence, my life seems more full of pleasure.

When I apply the accordion exercise to my subjective experience of the accident, I discover that my image is of being invaded, of being helpless, while at the same time other muscles resist. I organize this resistance more by assuming my fighting stance: I tighten my belly, clench my fist, breathe more rapidly, focus my eyes, and prepare to strike. I am able to disorganize this stance by slowly letting go of my muscle tensions, step by step, and not all at once, by breathing deep and slower. My chest tensions recede, my belly swells, my feet get hot. My experience is that when I disorganize the warrior stance, I also disorganize the helpless stance. I feel a pause which frequently gives me different perceptions of what is happening. While the warrior is still there to be called upon, I have a more gentle way to organize myself.

I now have the opportunity for more choices. I am not locked into one response pattern. I become aware in everyday life that there is no "right answer" and I can move in a direction without being compulsive about it. The realization that I could not entirely control my environment or what happened to me shook me to my core. I am learning to reorganize without a demand to perform.

When the collision returns to my awareness, I no longer try to suppress it. I experience the rerun as a total bodily event, not just something coming out of of my head. These reruns can occur at any time. There must be a somatic part of myself that retains the whole story and forces it to the surface of my conscious mind. I move into the warrior stance to avoid the helplessness when the rerun appears. Occasionally, when I drive by the place where the wreck took place, all my muscles respond as if another collision were going to happen. I re-enter the fight/flight situation. I now am able to reorganize this response fairly quickly when I recognize that it is occurring. These changes come and go; the old ways do not vanish. On top of the old ways, I perceive myself as building something new. The old ways are becoming less dominant. I experience my process somewhat like an archeological dig where one finds remnants of civilization, one on top of the other. Although the old bodily forms and states of mind reassert themselves, I am organizing a more receptive stance. I need less to be a performer and hero. I feel the ability to reform my life stance as an exhilarating new aspect of my existence.

Melissa: An Adultified Child

Melissa is an adultified child. She seems to have two bodies. Her lower half is unformed, small, undifferentiated. Her pelvis is pulled back with a lumbar lordosis somewhat like a young child's. Her upper body is rigid and spastic and appears to be under tremendous pressure.

Melissa was abused by her father and neglected by her mother. Her exterior is frozen and reflects the terror and hurt that occur when contact and comfort are withheld from a child. Melissa is hibernating, waiting for liberation.

She writes of her experience:
I was physically abused over a long period of time by my father. This occurred from the time I was an infant until I was six or seven. My father would hold down my arms, heap verbal abuse on me, and scream a lot. I cried for my mother but she never helped me. She made excuses for my father, telling me that I was naughty. I found out later that she agreed with my father that I was bad and uncontrollable.

The effects of this abuse remain with me to the present. I feel like a small child hiding inside an adult body, inadequate as a grownup yet pretending I am. I need help but find it difficult to ask. Over the past five years I have experienced a variety of illnesses — bronchitis, muscular spasms, pleurisy, weakness, and a great deal of chest pain. I have had a fast-growing, intrauterine tumor.

I experience myself as braced and rigid with an accompanying collapse in the middle. In order to survive, I stiffened myself and cut off my feelings and memories. For me, bracing is a preparation for a terrible onslaught. It also numbs my feelings and makes it possible to stand them. Bracing shuts off my awareness and cuts me off from the ouside world. I do not hear, I do not see, I no longer remember. When I brace I lock my knees, elbows, and shoulders and squeeze my brain. I know there is no help to be had. In my joints I cry out for real help. If I become rigid, I will no longer be present and neither will the terror.

I experience myself as braced most of the time in relation to other people and to my own thoughts and ideas. I expect to be assaulted. I frequently discover that I put up with abusive situations which other people would not tolerate for a second. But for me, exploitation is normal. I construct barriers between myself and a world which I view as hell, as a place of torture, a place I live but do not participate in. I am survival-oriented, determined to stay alive and function in some way. My memory is weak, my thinking is rigid. While I know things intellectually, I do not feel them.

As I look back on my childhood, I recall how terrorized and paralyzed I was. I am still a terrorized child. I cannot seem to grow up and shake it off. I experienced despair because nothing I did could stop the abuse. There was no one to turn to for help, no one else

Melissa
Terror, Abuse, Helplessness

Melissa is unbounded and collapsed in her lower half while her neck and head are rigid. She appears to have two bodies. This pattern is a response to neglect and early abandonment. The upper part is pushing the lower part away so as not to be overwhelmed. Melissa's self-image is polarized between weak and strong.

Melissa's neck is overextended and stiff. Her head, digestive tube and trachea are spastic and elongated, distancing her head and brain from her torso. Her lungs are deflated which reduces her breathing. She has poor muscle tone in her abdomen and pelvis which contribute to reduced feeling and a lack of gendered identity.

would stop my father and neither could I. As I became desperate, I would try to cling to my mother but she would respond with anger. I lost my sense of reality and came to hate myself because I could not function very well. Most of the time I was frightened. I found school difficult and making friends impossible. I was quite desperate but did not know why. Because I could not comprehend, I was anguished. I had no sense of myself. I still lack trust for others, have little positive regard for myself, and a fear and distaste for intimate relationships. I experience a constant pervasive sense of terror.

I organize myself by bracing, locking my knees, elbows, wrists, ankles, shoulders, neck—all my joints. My breathing is shallow and confined to the upper torso. I contract my muscles as much as possible in order to shut off feeling and limit my awareness. When I practice the accordion exercise, I intensify these patterns in stages and allow my rigidity and contractions to become less intense. I sometimes experience a pause which allows a different set of experiences and memories to arise. Occasionally, I experience pulsation. I try to identify with this new feeling state with my emotions and body. The accordion exercise of expansion and contraction sometimes reduces my feeling of being a victim. When I can identify my response, I have a means of gently restructuring it.

Originally, my rigidity and bracing cut me off from feeling or being aware of the abuse; now I become rigid when anything remotely reminds me of the past. When I organize and disorganize my rigidity, I can slowly experience how devastasting the abuse was. Even today I cannot allow the full force of it into my awareness. Organization and disorganization, the accordion exercise, begins to break the chain of events and gives my deep internal system a chance for a new response. It is quite wonderful when I discover that many of the negative responses I make really are learned and so can be changed. I can find new means of expression and experience my past as flashbacks rather than something which has present meaning for me.

I am often surprised to find out how injured I was. The idea of being an injured person has not been a vivid concept to me. As I am able to see the levels of my injury, I also see the possibility for wholeness in a different way. I find that disorganizing my response pattern allows me to brace a little less in relationships with others. As I brace less, a little more of my feeling comes up. I sometimes get a sense of a truer part of myself which I trust very deeply.

A Somatic-Emotional Procedure to Disorganize an Insult

My clinical experience teaches me that people are often unaware of how they use or misuse themselves. They are unconscious of their somatic-emotional state and unaware of how they fragment feeling from action or ideas and emotions. The way a person organizes his response is an innate process; he uses himself in a particular way yet does not experience how he does this. This is the real clinical problem. Therefore I set about to develop a methodology to help a person learn about how he uses himself and how his insult pattern is organized. When I use this procedure in my private practice or with a group of clients, I heighten the pattern of stress to see how it is organized in layers, muscular and emotional postures, ideas and images, feelings and actions. I want individuals to reconstitute their stress patterns and gradually intensify and deintensify them. Once they experience their somatic-emotional pattern, they can begin to deconstitute it.

A basic insult pattern is not necessarily disorganized by talking about feelings or memories, encouraging emotional catharsis, or engaging in visualization and recategorization. These approaches might offer relief, provide insight, enable a client to take a distance, even to behave differently, but they do not disorganize the way a person has embodied his pattern of insult. The somatic-emotional exercises I have developed bring the stress pattern to the foreground and show how commands are organized into actions. The muscle-emotional-brain continuum operates by shades of pressure, expansion and contraction. It is the base for emotional posture and action. As a person identifies with his organizing pattern, he discovers his accompanying projections of feelings, images, ideas, emotions, and actions.

Somatic-emotional exercises are based upon the accordion procedure of expansion and contraction, organization and disorganization, intensification and deintensification: do it more, wait, do it more, wait, do it less, pause, do it still less. These exercises instruct a person in how he uses himself and teach him how to learn and use what he learns. They also provide a means to undo reflex responses, to connect muscular patterns to emotional states and their accompanying images and thoughts, and to restore a basic somatic-emotional way of being in the world.

Using the somatic-emotional procedure, a person reorganizes his pattern of insult by calling it forth, layer by layer, until all the deep muscle structures reveal their part. It is much like turning a screw. A move in one direction or the other will tighten or loosen. Similarly, once a person learns how his insult pattern is organized, he can begin to disorganize and reorganize it.

The accordion practice of organization and disorganization focuses attention on that aspect of the muscle contraction-relaxation reflex that an individual has some control over. The command—do it more, do it still more, do it less—permits a person to undo what it is he is doing; he can learn to disorganize what he has just organized. Muscular contraction extends the antagonists of the same muscle group; the stretch reflex demands that these extended muscles begin to contract. These procedures create a slower rhythm than a person is usually accustomed to. This slow motion gives a different sense of time and allows the slower acting muscles to dominate the quick red-fibered action muscles. A tidal experience of rhythmic pulsation grows and instructs the cortex in the person's basic rhythms—extension, expansion, pause, withdrawal, contraction, pause. Experience is layered; a person sees he has an interior and a depth as well as a surface and an exterior.

Somatic-emotional exercises change the state that a person is in and encourage the return of basic pulsation, the rhythmic visceral expansion and contraction of feeling. This cycle of peristalsis gives an inner warmth in the viscera and a sense of an interior or a center. It also generates information from which feeling images grow and organizes a biochemical state of existence, for example, pleasure. When the state in which a person lives is changed, his value system changes as well.

What a person forms can be unformed, each layer can be disorganized and reorganized. An exercise evokes a person's form, then asks him to create more form or to undo the form he has created. Learning the control of one's self in both directions enables an individual to live with the continuum of his feelings, sensations, and associations. He deepens his self-perception, self-mastery, and self-possession. More importantly, he learns how form and forming works and how to deprogram and disorganize an insult state that remains deeply embedded. Once a person reconstitues his insult pattern and learns how it is formed, he becomes able to contain the associated feelings and memories, reorganize his state, and form a self.

Rigidity and Spasticity

When I work with certain clients who are rigid and spastic, I want them to reconstitute their pattern of bracing against pain, then experience the multiple layers and see what state it organizes. The function of rigidity and spasticity is to provide protection and a feeling of powerfulness. But it does not end there. As form becomes squeezed and tight, living space becomes smaller and less available. Alarm increases muscle tone. It begins with a stage of alertness and deepens, by degrees, into rigidity and spasticity. This pattern originates in the upper body, neck, mouth, eyes, and especially in the hands and fingers.

In working with a client who has these patterns, I might ask him to sit up, put his arms at his sides, and stretch into his fingers intensely, stretching them as much as he can. I would ask him to repeat this pattern of stretching and slowly releasing several times. I want him to experience his rigidity and overboundedness and become aware of how it spreads into his forearms, shoulders, spine, legs, chest and head. I want him to discover how much of his total organization is involved and how deep it goes.

I then turn the client's attention to the emotional qualities of his somatic pattern. I ask, what kind of experience begins to grow in him? Does he feel detached and numb? Does his organism begin to squeeze itself into two dimensions? Does his rigidity make him detached, beside himself, separated, dissociated? The person may begin to recognize these phases.

Next, I might ask him to stiffen his hands again and press his arms close to his sides and feel the conflict between trying to breathe and stiffening his arms. His throat may close or constrict. Can he experience the rigidity spreading from his arms to his face and mouth and down his throat into his chest? Does it extend into his legs and feet? He can practice disorganizing the pattern gradually, first in his legs, then in his abdomen, his chest, throat, face, head, shoulders, arms, and finally, his hands. I would repeat this procedure of rigidifying and releasing several times so that the client experiences more of his process and how it affects his total organism.

What does the rigidity organize emotionally and cognitively? Is his danger perceived as coming from the outside or his are his own impulses perceived as the enemy? An increase in aliveness demands a response, yet sensations can be a danger against which a person rigidifies. When the client releases these rigidities, he may be flooded with sensations and memories which he has been defending against.

This simple exercise, using the hands and arms, reconstitutes a rigid person's primary startle response. By repeating the exercise, by disorganizing in stages, and by discovering the thoughts, feelings, and images that emerge, the client's state becomes his teacher. He experiences how he creates his spastic pattern of being in the world and can recognize and disorganize aspects of it that continue as he goes about his daily life.

Pulling Up, Surprise, Dread

Some people respond to an insult by making a boundary to keep others away. They establish an inner psychological state of distance. When a person with this pattern disorganizes, caution and fear may emerge. He may be in a conflict between action and perception, between pulling back and pushing away. The struggle between attack and withdrawal determines how he is in the world, the form he assumes, and how he thinks and feels about himself.

With this insult pattern I ask the client to sit in a chair, bend his elbows and place the back of his hands on his chest with his palms facing out, and extend into his fingers. This gives him the feeling of getting ready to push an object away or to resist something or someone. I tell him to move his hands and arms six inches forward and to say out loud, "Stay there!" He may repeat this exercise several times—intensifying and releasing it—until he experiences the contraction in his forearms, biceps, shoulders and neck. Gradually pressuring all the muscle segments, the surprise pattern is invoked. The person does not relax or give the pattern up, but disorganizes it step by step. Surprise might become concern, and then fear.

This position of surprise, caution, warding something off, pushing something away affects the person's thinking and his mood. I would have the person repeat this pushing away stance using his arms and hands and focus on his emotional expressions of suspicion, anger, and fear. As he invokes the entire pattern, in the hands and fingers, the feet and legs, the neck, head, jaw, and abdomen and buttocks, does he become terrified? Does he pull himself inwards and upwards and enter into deep shock and hibernation? Does he numb himself to play dead?. Do his thoughts race? Does he have expectations of catastrophe? Is he submissive to some fate? Is he in the past or the present? Does he experience himself as small and childlike or big and adult?

The purpose of invoking the pushing-away pattern is for a client to feel his pattern of making boundaries, how deep this pattern runs, how it is organized step by step, layer by layer, and how to use the experience of organization to disorganize it. As he experiences the multiple levels of his pushing-away pattern (caution, submission, terror, deep shock, and hibernation, and the accompanying somatic organization) the person discovers which parts are no longer necessary and begins to make boundaries that are appropriate to the moment.

Startle, Surprise and Stiffening

A startle pattern is layered and involves a sequence of muscular, organismic contractions which range from mild bracing and heightened alertness to the spasm of terror. As a response to insult is reorganized over and over again, it becomes deeply embedded in a person's bodied life. Since the insult pattern is ongoing at the deepest level of the muscular network it is, in fact, an automatic emotional stance which becomes intensified when invoked in the present. It is often difficult to break such a fixed response pattern into its sequences of movement. When I work with someone who is locked into an automatic response to insult, I want him to experience the layers of organization in his pattern and the sequence involved in going from A to B.

I ask a client to lay on a bed, put his arms at his sides, palms facing inwards, and to begin to stiffen or stretch his arms and hands. I have him repeat this slowly several times until he begins to have some sense of the overall pattern. As he stiffens and releases I ask him to say out loud, "be careful," "watch out," or "don't do that." In this way he can begin to grasp how his first stiffening contraction intensifies to spasm and the in-between stages. As we repeat this emotional posture and reconstitute the pattern, I try to get him to experience the levels, layers, and structure of his response and the differences between an initial challenge and a fixed spasm.

As he moves back and forth between bracing and rigidity, I call his attention to the different layers of his experience—what is happening in his throat and jaw, arms and shoulders, chest and belly, mouth, eyes and head, and his legs and feet. I want him to pause at each place so that his organismic experience can imprint his brain. I want him to experience how a little bit of stiffness is linked with "caution," an increase in organization with "watch out," and a total spasm with "get away," as well as all his psychological and emotional associations.

As he differentiates the layers of organization involved in stiffening, I then turn his attention to the feeling qualities of his experience and his accompanying images. I may ask him some of the following: "What kind of alertness do you experience? What is it like to still yourself? How does the pattern of investigation differ from caution or from immobilization? What are your accompanying feelings and thoughts? Have you become numb? What is it like to disassociate from the rest of yourself? What do you have to do to put up with something that you cannot get away from? As you slowly disorganize the spasm involved in 'get away,' and return to 'watch out,' and then to 'caution' is there a flood of associations and feelings? Do you experience a different level of excitation?"

With the organization and disorganization of stiffening the arms and hands, I want the client to experience all levels of recall—motoric, visceral, images, and organismic. Catharsis may be called for, but, in and of itself, it does not end the spasm. Disorganization and emotional response does. That is what healing is all about.

Conflict and Confusion

A person's previous insult pattern may act as a barrier to his present self-contact or his ongoing contact with others. When he is approached by another he feels uncomfortable. While there is no outward reason to feel threatened, still he experiences being on guard. He feels suspicious, fearful, or angry rather than expectant, curious, and full of interest. His old insult pattern is not forgotten but functions as an organismic-emotional reminder that he may be insulted again. The present situation is misread and the individual automatically invokes a pattern of attack, turning away, or submission that is uncalled for.

When I work with a person with these patterns, I want him to focus on the relationship between his head and his torso and to determine when his forward glance becomes turning away. I have him lay on a bed, tighten the back of his neck and jaw, isolating his head from his neck and his chest from his abdomen. I have him repeat this process in gradual stages, each time tightening and stiffening his head and jaw so that he experiences how he makes an internal distance. As he repeats this exercise, I call his attention to what he is doing in his tongue, neck, nose, chin, palate, eyes, diaphragm, and belly. I ask him to see what it means to take a distance from himself and how his experience changes as he disorganizes the multiple layers of his pattern. As he grasps how he separates his belly from his chest and his chest from his head, I suggest he make a slight twist as if to turn away. I then ask what part of himself turns away and if it is countered by another part which insists on still facing forward.

As we continually intensify and disorganize the distancing and turning away in stages, I suggest that the person identify different states with the feelings of dislike, repugnance, and revulsion. Is a little bit of distancing associated with dislike, more distance with repugnance, and turning away with revulsion? Does this distancing give a feeling of superiority? Does he begin to dismiss his experience or the other? At what point does contempt or moral superiority enter in? What happens to his breathing? Does it shift from the belly to the chest? What are the different feelings associated with each of these places?

I want him to link his organismic experience with his feelings and his associations. I encourage him to explore the relationship between reflex and the volitional, the autonomic and the manageable. Distancing and turning away invokes a reflex. What he does is already going on. Then he amplifies it. As he does this slowly and in stages, there is a relationship between what is given and how he is increasing it. He creates a different relationship between the volitional and nonvolitional, among his cortex, midbrain, and hindbrain. These are the levels of his self-dialogue. He can take the sensation and the experience somatically, link it with his associations and feelings, and deal with them motorically and symbolically. Somatic identification increases as his conflict pattern becomes more vivid, he grasps experientially that there is more than one level to his existence, and finds a somatic-emotional way to reform it.

Patterns of Distress / 54

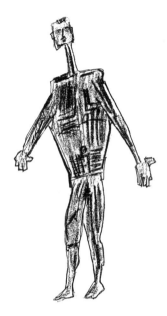

Rigid, Dense, Stiffened

Depressed, Collapsed

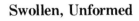

Swollen, Unformed

Fragmented   **Dense, Weak**

55 / *Patterns of Distress*

Dense, Rigid

Rigid, Collapsed

Rigid, Split

Rigid, Weak

Clinical Philosophy and Practical Insights

It is essential that a clinician understand the body as a process when he begins to enter the somatic basis of his client's existence. To ask someone to move in a certain way, to alter his breathing, to evoke his excitatory pattern is, in fact, to enter into the ground floor of existence. A person's responses should be viewed with respect since many of them do not easily fit into categories, but, rather, describe something that is profoundly personal. A person's responses seek a direction for his form. Dreams, excitatory patterns, urges, memories and gestures, seek not merely emotional or verbal articulations of deep-rooted pain, but, in fact, to shape a form, an organization.

When a therapist addresses tensions and contractions, he enters an organization that has maintained a particular life expression over a continuous period of time. This life organization has a unique set of rules. A posture is much more than a defense or a response to a childhood insult. It represents the collection of all the experiences of a person's life up until the present moment, organized into a posture that reflects his experience. When a clinician begins a therapeutic or educational process, he enters into how anatomy as a living, dynamic expression of existence forms, deforms, and reforms itself. A childhood insult is nothing more than an internal or external obstacle organized as a living expression with its own rules. Whether he uses massage, rolfing, kicking, breathing, stretching or the somatic-emotional exercises I have developed, a clinician begins to learn something about how a person shapes himself, what his rules are, and what form he is trying to maintain.

In my language, this describes the formative process, those rules of organization which take the given elements of creation and the unique aspects of individual socialization and combine them to make a particular body. These rules are built into every single cell of a person's existence and transmit that information as a collective unit to the whole organism. This process of organization is what a clinician or somatic educator works with; he is working with a person's life.

Until a client recognizes that there is a larger organization behind his feelings, thinking, and action, he will either identify solely with his feelings or else with his therapist in some way. In therapy, as a client learns that there is more than his feelings, a dialogue to connect him to his forming process can begin. I ask a client, "How do you organize your feelings? What pattern or shape do they take? What do you want to do with them?" With these questions, I focus a client's feelings and his cognition of them and help him to reorganize a form. When a client is identified too strongly with his feelings alone, he struggles to find meaning in them and may miss the whole pattern of their organization. Feeling and organizing action are the key, not feeling and interpretation.

A somatic-emotional solution to clinical dilemmas differs from standard therapeutic assumptions. Although it is essential to change the client's inner state, it is not enough. The emphasis in formative psychology is to identify and to sustain the organizing process of the client. The task is to grasp how a client tries to use himself. What is the actual language by which the client carries out a dialogue between his feeling and his knowing? The brain does not keep track only of what is going on but HOW it is going on. There is a series of inner communications that give rise to a person's various feelings and the messages, associations, and actions that accompany them. These messages occur as sensations, behavioral gestures, organ movements and language. If a person is willing to engage in formative experience, the organism will always respond, to the best of its ability, to reveal structure and its process of shaping. A client can keep repeating a stereotyped piece of behavior, or he can use his experience to organize himself. Every situation, therefore, represents a possibility as a formative stimulus.

A tissue state implies learning on the cellular level. The geometry of the neural system, how different tracks become compacted or separated, is involved. In technical terms it is called neurobiotaxis or the elongation of axons or the current stimulation in the geometric pattern of how cell bodies are laid out and fired up in a pattern. Some therapists, educators, and parents do not understand metabolic disparity. A neural impulse travels 400 feet a second if the pathway is direct. There is a simple reflex arc going from the surface back into the spinal axis and out again at the motor end. Once it enters the midbrain, the impulse narrows itself and is forced through the pons into a surface area that is greater. What has previously traveled at a certain rate must now go over a longer distance, therefore there is a discrepancy between arousal and response. Therapeutically, this implies that verbal interaction has to wait for a shift downward which converts insight into feeling and cellular change. Somatic work directly arouses the body and moves this arousal to the other structures in order to create symbolic and feeling behavioral organization.

The Five Steps

A formative therapist continually invokes the client's ability to find a behavioral pattern by asking him the question, "How do you do that?" Generally, there are five steps to the answer. The five steps are: (1) the body/emotional stance; (2) how the person organizes his stance; (3) how he disorganizes his stance; (4) how he remains unorganized; (5) and, finally, how he reorganizes. This process is going on all the time. Each one of these stages represents an attempt to maintain or vivify form or disorganize form and then reorganize it. These five steps involve a dialogue where the process talks to itself about changing directions and altering its metabolism.

Between step two and step three is the struggle between organization and the fight for disorganization. In a normal life, organization gives a person form, moves him towards a cohesive expressive system, and takes him through biological and psychological growth patterns. In going from one somatic-emotional shape to another shape, something has to be disrupted, taken down, changed and reincorporated. To some people this basic truth about change is threatening. In every organism, there is a struggle going on inside between form and reforming.

I had a patient who, as a child, was fed every three or four hours regardless of whether he was crying or not. If he cried, he was not to be touched or comforted. He could only be touched at the appropriate time. By compacting himself, he learned to defend himself against the anxiety of waiting as well as his impulses of hunger. In working to disorganize his compactness, anxiety emerged. This anxiety was related to his feelings of hunger, a trigger that made him feel that he was going to lose control. Hunger and appetite were the signal to become dense. Because hunger meant longing, appetite itself was the trigger for increased organization. The highly dense structure warded off his own hunger. I wanted this client to recognize the quality of his compact organization. I wanted him to learn how much contact he could manage before he would get out of control.

The somatic-emotional exercises given in this book help to identify and disorganize patterns of insult. They change the state that a person is in and encourage the return of basic pulsation. The pulsatory continuum is the rhythmic visceral expansion and contraction of feeling. This cycle of peristalsis gives a feeling of inner warmth in the viscera and a sense of an interior or a center. It also generates information from which feeling images grow and organizes a biochemical state of existence, for example, pleasure. Pleasure is a biproduct of a peristaltic wave. When the state in which a person lives is changed, his value system changes as well.

Working with a client's formative process is very much like being a parent. A good parent represents a more mature nervous system than the child's, therefore he serves as a boundary until the child's own system develops. A good parent knows the right time to put the child to bed before the child starts to nod off. A somatic therapist functions the same way with a client. Often, he sits back and does nothing but act as a boundary. I start with the basic premise: less is more. When there is a clear indication that the experience is assimilated, it is appropriate to go the next step.

Once a client has some self-management over his insult pattern, the pulsatory state which emerges allows him to root himself in his own nature. He forms a relationship with that which generates his excitatory and symbolic life. Grounding is more than encouraging sensations in the lower limbs of the client. Grounding is a change in the tissue state which generate the feelings and images of life. Somatic therapy brings about a change in the tissue which then has to be supported and formed into self-identity and action. This new organization allows a form to emerge which reflects the experience. This basic tissue state is an urge to live as well as a feeling of life that seeks to form a personal shape.

These understandings make working with clients easier. The organizing and disorganizing process is exactly what the client experiences and is what a somatic therapist works with. What is the feeling form? What is disorganizing? What wants to reorganize? How does a person live this or flee it? What wants to reorganize?

A somatic therapist enters directly into the client's process. He gets the client to express, in the language of his organism, the way he moves himself and talks about himself—the history of his experience on a cellular and emotional level. The client's struggle is with a cellular memory. For example, he may have wanted support himself but had to give support to his parents in the hope that they would give it back to him. The client's personal unconcious, in the form of a motor memory, comes to the fore, and then finds a way to bring into play the verbal and pictoral introjects that society gave in the form of language. A somatic therapist helps the client form a new relationship to his early experience of insult by providing a human dimension to talk about his pain and his inability to organize a response to that pain.

The layers of cellular organization are a basic construct of what some call the unconcious. A person does not pull a symbolic form out or a memory bank and say I remember this or that. Somatic work links the cortical or brain areas of symbols to motor action, and turns them into feeling forms, so that mental symbols really represent cellular and feeling states.

How I Work With A Client

I am always interested in the image that the client presents, how it is structured, what is being organized and disorganized, and what form this serves. I start out by trying to understand the organization a person has.

In conducting an interview with a person, I ask what is the precipitating crisis that brings him into my office. I then begin to pay attention to his shape, where is he refusing to change shape, and how he has difficulty conceptualizing or making transitions. Most importantly, I look for how he uses himself—is he overdramatic or is he shy—and how, exactly, he does this. Then I look for the body shape that reflects his state. I note the way he uses language as he describes what happened to him. How he uses language may tell me about the nature of his reactions—dark, slippery, wet, dry, thick, spacious, dense, compact, burning, hot, tingling, pulsating. All these qualities are expressions of the organism.

My way of working is to understand where a person is in any organization or situation. What is the situation? What is undergoing disorganization? What is undergoing reorganization? What are the discrepancies between what needs to be organized versus what needs to be disorganized? I begin to identify the major areas where he is under or over organized. As the client learns about the organization of his experience, he can then pay attention to how that learning will move him toward another form and enable him to disorganize his present one.

I try to identify the person's structure and its function. For example, a swollen structure has no inner organization. Such a person is organized on the surface. He is always engaged in the process of incorporating the other. Either he takes him in and uses him or he enters into the other. A therapeutic task with a swollen person is to build an internal structure. The swollen structure should practice being dense and rigid and begin to organize boundaries. A swollen structure is a result of a breakdown in the developmental process. The child either did not receive enough interaction, or he received too much. Everything was done for him, he never developed boundaries and resistance. A person who has been overprotected needs to establish boundaries and to meet challenges. Overprotected types are good at getting others to do things for them, and their challenge is how to organize away from sloth.

I frequently ask the question, "Tell me what you do and how you do it?" I want to know what a client does, how he makes himself dense, or how he inflates himself. With a collapsed structure, I want a client to experience how he deflates and then inflates himself. Then he can begin to organize a structure that represents his real size. I want him to practice being bigger with a structure that is built from within. I want to soften dense and rigid structures to see how each will disorganize, and how they will reorganize a softer, more flexible form.

Forming, the process of organizing, is satisfying even though it may not deliver pleasure. I try to get my clients to perceive what satisfaction is and to organize themselves for longer term goals and sustain them. Experiencing the satisfaction of endurance is its own reward and differs from seeking pleasure in the future or hoping for pleasure as the price of endurance.

I try to help people form something from their experiences, either internally or externally. Either I assist them to use the experience they have, or I help them create a certain layer of experience that they are missing. For example, a person can learn to use his brain and muscles to move from controlling himself, to managing himself, to forming himself. This involves three separate forms.

Less is more. How a person uses his experience is the clue to how much contact or intimacy he wants. Arousal and excitation are a very small part of the continuum of the experience of self-forming. They are, in fact, the smallest part of that experience. Vitality and aliveness cannot and should not be defined on an arousal/excitatory continuum.

Organization versus Disorganization

There are two fundamental reactions to stimuli. The first is an increase in activity, the second a decrease in activity. These changes are based on the reflex arc, the sensory and synaptic motor end or an amoebic movement of the cell wall. Every organism has its rhythm of moving out and coming back. Either there will be an increase in the expansion movement or an increase in the withdrawal movement—an increase in activity or a decrease in activity, an increase in organization or a decrease in organization. So there are multiple possibilities: overbounded and overactive, overbounded and underactive, underbounded and overactive, underbounded and underactive. These are different responses to challenge, an increase in organization or activity or a decrease in organization or activity.

A therapist needs to know which aspect of the organizing/disorganizing process he is going to invoke. With rigid and dense clients, he is going to emphasize the disorganizing part and encourage those places where there is the least amount of form, Step 1 and Step 4. The goal is to soften the overbounded structure. With weak or swollen structures, a therapist wants to encourage organization which he does by emphasizing Step 3 and Step 2. A therapist would not say to a swollen structure, "disorganize and let go", since it is not useful for unbounded structures to become involuntary.

A formative therapist helps generate and sustain the basic process of aliveness, the powerful pulsatory waves that are expressed as excitation and feeling. These feelings give a sense of vigor to a person's thinking, acting, social relationships, and work. The somatic therapist, using somatic emotional methods, seeks to know and help the organism form these patterns of vitality into a personal form.

Catharsis versus Self-Management

When a therapist encourages a client to stop whatever it is he is doing and sit back, sooner or later an involuntary movement will start. The therapist then observes its organization and spread. At what point does the person become overwhelmed by forces that he perceives as alien or outside of himself? Is his response to give in to the involuntary experience, to become cathartic? My therapeutic goal is to teach self-management, not catharsis. I would ask a cathartic client, "Where did you go and what did you learn?" Many people who are cathartic lack thought; they have a high degree of responsiveness and excitability and are capable of throwing themselves into an activity. At the same time, they are not able to use their cathartic experience to form a more satisfying life or human relationships. What good does it do a client to move freely if, in fact, he cannot be social with others?

Catharsis does not equal freedom although the promise of freedom is contained in the idea of catharsis. It is not the central point of the healing endeavor. Catharsis may help a client relieve emotional pressure or restore basic emotional expressions such as sadness or anger. It also may overwhelm the organism and create disorganization.

Although it can be important to experience intense excitement, unbridled emotions, and spontaneous moments, a person can fall into an impulsive pattern of disorganization. The heart of human life is the individual's ability to form his experiences into appropriate personalized expression. Larry Bird, the basketball player, exemplifies this. He has a natural talent, but his talent is rehearsed and practiced over and over and over again, until he has a very complicated, imaginative, motoric, feeling, sensing organization that is responsive. Every error he makes is analyzed in relationship to a failure of coordination that has to be integrated. This is true for all of us. Successful intra or interpersonal relationships do not just happen. We have to actively participate in the shaping of our relationships and lives. This is a creative process.

Joan: Family Illness

Joan is a short, pear-shaped woman with a large abdomen. She is round of form and weak and undifferentiated in her muscular connective tissue. She has strong emotional responses, but is weak in action, impulsive and not in control.

The threatened loss of a family member challenged her identity as a mother and also triggered a deep helplessness linked to her early life, when she was an abandoned child. One pattern was already in place, only to be intensified by the present shock and trauma. Her early bonding and nurturing was halted when she was placed in an institution for children. She suffered infant depression. Later, with foster parents, Joan was continually neglected and felt a lack of intimacy and real mothering. She needed contact yet the outside did not respond. Her own internal impulses and needs became an insult that threatened her organization.

Joan's current feelings of helplessness do not come solely from the present situation of her child's illness. Since her ability to bond and separate was aborted in childhood and adolescence, every threat of loss becomes a shock. Her need to belong, her ability to manage her own impulses, her need to be in control are threatened. She feels humiliated and helpless and wants to withdraw into depression.

Joan writes:

About five years ago, as I was entering middle age, my grownup child was discovered to have a serious illness. I went into a deep shock for about three months, followed by two years of on-again, off-again depression.

When I first received the news, I was shocked, went numb, and wanted to hibernate. I felt everything around me happening in slow motion. I experienced dissociation and disorientation. Later, I began to feel helpless and hopeless. Then my long-standing depression, a feeling left over from being abandoned at birth, returned.

I gained thirty pounds in a short period as if to give myself a protective covering. I obsessively fantasized about loss and what I would

65 / Patterns of Distress

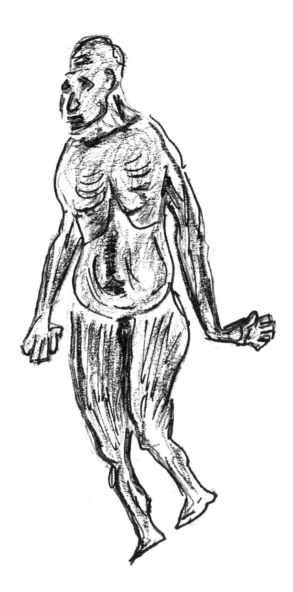

Joan
Hopelessness, Despair, Hibernation

Joan has a weak outer structure with a lowered center of gravity that threatenes to engulf her rational process and her strong inner organ motility. She is an unformed adult, a child seeking a container. Joan is a victim of neglect, a lack of interaction which resulted in the shrinking of the muscles of self-containment.

do if I lost everyone and everything. I began to create more distance from those who were close to me.

Somatically, I braced and collapsed, accompanied by a pulling-in. The pulling-in is related to losing everything and feeling that I must protect myself, be alert, focus, wait and hold my ground. Bracing is preparing myself as if to receive a blow. I sense an angry, frightening presence preparing to attack. My feeling is one of danger, preparing to fight or run. In collapsing I experience the loss of everything, I become a sorrowful presence, hopeless, helpless, giving up.

What I experienced could be metaphorically compared to a major earthquake occurring along an existing fault line. My original insult, the loss of my natural parents at birth, carried through my life with a series of aftershocks—an unhappy childhood, a permanent separation from my foster parents, divorce from my husband, a long experience as a single parent, the departure of my children from home to start their own lives. Therefore, I go through or am put through continuous situations which reinforce my pulled-in, braced, collapsed way of functioning. I feel my self-image crumble, implode and explode, as if I am nothing but a small speck.

My reaction to my child's illness was to mentally slow down, decrease my attention span, lose my ability to concentrate. Emotionally I began to lose interest in life, to become indifferent towards my surroundings and myself, and to physically collapse. My subjective experience was of being completely alone, except for God and nature. I experienced myself withdrawing from the world. I was angry with God but did not experience being abandoned in return. I was thrown headlong back into my experiences as a child and my own belief in my sturdiness came into question.

I began to use the accordion exercise to work with my helplessness, and discovered that I organized myself by standing still, holding my breath, clenching my fists, rigidifying my spine, and slightly hunching my shoulders to brace myself. I disorganized this by lowering my head, breathing, feeling into my belly, keeping my feet flat on the floor, bringing my shoulders slightly back, unclenching my fists, and slightly bending my knees to release some of the tension in my spine. I experienced a wave of pulsation and allowed this warmth and motility to move outward and upward, filling my inner space with an inwardness that was missing

When I feel helpless, I rigidify so I will not collapse. Doing the accordion exercise helps me to move out of my rigidity and gives me the range of movement from rigidity to collapse so that I can find a place in the accordion where I can live without being caught in the extremes. I run through the accordion over and over and then pause as a new way to form myself begins. This exercise becomes the container by which I can practice new and different responses and learn self-control. I believe the changes that they bring about are building blocks. The smaller the change, the longer it lasts. This small change can be integrated into a repertoire of existing behavior fairly easily and becomes the seed for further changes. My initial response to any insult is to withdraw and isolate myself. With the accordion exercise I get a different inner sense and feeling which enables me to re-establish contact with others.

In the recent threat to my family, my challenge was to disorganize the shock and disbelief meant to protect and numb me from the experience. My extreme startle response froze me and slowed down time. My challege is to reconnect with myself and to re-enter time and life. By disorganizing the frozen stillness, I make contact with myself at the deepest level. I invoke a pulsatory movement in my belly and pelvis that spreads throughout my body. My hope for the future is no longer a mental image, but a sensation of my own tissue aliveness, a feeling that is familiar and reassuring.

Clinical Comment: In my work with Joan, I focused on two aspects. One was to investigate her pattern of depression, its organization and its function by using exercises to sharpen and bring into focus her depressive structure. These exercises established an inner feeling of self-control and alleviated her sense of helplessness. Being with her, sharing her fear of loss, my presence acted as a boundary that she could learn to accept and take from. I also encouraged her to form contraction patterns to contain her pelvic and thoracic pulsations. She was able to contain an increased vitality that gave her an inner structure somatically and psychologically. She could be in herself as well as in her environment.

Jacob: Grief and Despair

Jacob is a rigid, stiff, athletic person whose somatic shape is a combination of collapsed, rigid, and fragmented. His body is twisted as if he is going forward with one side and ahead with the other. His head sits on his neck somewhat askew, tilted and turned as if it does not belong to him. On one side he looks adult, on the other, small, helpless, and immature. When he speaks he often appears confused.

When Jacob's father died suddenly during his adolescence, his disbelief left him feeling stiff and frozen. He entered a depressive state that lasted for some time. Later, Jacob received shock treatments to deal with his depression. These treatments fragmented him, dissociating him from his depression but not disorganizing it.

Jacob's pattern of insult is layered. At the deepest level is his frozen grief, then his depressive reaction, then his fragmentation caused by electric shock. He cannot hold himself together under a buildup of excitatory or emotional pressure.

Jacob describes his state:
Two major events occurred in my life. The first, which happened between the ages of eleven and thirteen, involved the sudden illness and eventual death of my father whom I loved dearly. I became deeply despondent, I could not believe what had happened nor could I reorganize my life. I suffered from severe depression and eventually had to be hospitalized. There I received shock treatments. I lost my sense of identity, I could not remember my name or how old I was. To this day, I do not recall the exact number of treatments I received even though I have been told on a number of occasions.

My response to these twin events was initially disbelief which later turned into helplessness, hopelessness, and, finally, despair. I find myself perpetually braced with an added organization which pressures me to survive and to perform. Emotionally, I am in a continuous state of suspicion as if ready to receive a blow. Subjectively, this registers as a mild state of anxiety or a sense that some disaster is about to take place. When I set out to do something, I feel helpless. I tend to disorganize under stress. I believe I cannot trust myself and tend not to rely upon others or believe they will be there when I need them. I have not been able to establish a satisfying long-term relationship with a woman. I split women into friends, of whom I have many, and those who are lovers. When I try to combine the two, I become anxious and fear that something terrible will happen. I fear being a victim, having no power, or others taking advantage of me. I construct my stance to be like my father, a warrior and a performer, someone determined to be successful but fear I will die suddenly as he did. Over and over again, I prove that I can take on challenges, conquer, and survive. Yet, under stress, I disorganize and try to get others to help me so I will not collapse. I live the life of an outcast, never feeling I belong anywhere.

I experience physical and mental bracing, I contract and harden myself because of my earlier experiences. I believe that there is something wrong with me. Therefore, I tend to withdraw from others, hide myself, and become isolated and self-contained. I feel that the normal sequence of going from a young man, protected by his family, to manhood, moving out of the family gradually with their support, was denied to me by the difficult events of my adolescence.

To avoid being a victim, I brace and pull up to be a warrior. I squeeze my brain, tighten my neck and throat, harden my chest and

69 / Patterns of Distress

Jacob
Shock, Trauma, Abandonment

Jacob's pattern of avoidance and dissociation is brought about by loss, shock, and unfinished mourning. His structure is dense, compacted, fragmented, and segmented, attempts to ward off an inner pain of disbelief and grief.

back muscles while pulling my stomach in. When I intensify these actions, I begin to experience their disorganization. That place in between squeezing and total disorganization feels very good, a relief, a sense of reconnecting to myself, somewhat like a mild trance. When I am true to this feeling, I can create a new organization, I feel more connected to myself. I elongate my spine to support myself. When hardened, I experience myself as rigid and twisted. When I can undo this compactedness, I feel young and full of promise.

I now can recognize when I am in or going into my warrior stance. With this recognition, I can choose to be there or not. I become in charge of how I am in the world simply by how I organize and disorganize my somatic-emotional attitude. My feelings of despair, resignation, sadness, and loss are more under my own influence.

In the past, I have tried many things to relieve my memories of depression and shock treatments. Now when these feelings surface, I can relate to them differently. I feel like I am reforming my brain and not simply remembering as I did before. This process gives me a sense of being in charge of myself. I am able to create a peaceful and calm state in which I know what I want and do not want. The love I had toward my father is no longer a danger. I can form relationships with men that are not competitive or clinging. With women, I am beginning to form a link from head to heart. At work, I no longer push myself as hard. I reduce the excessive demands I make upon myself and organize a somatic state that does not involve stiffening and pressuring myself. I can just be and enjoy life rather than survive and perform. I have more contact with others. I am amazed that there is still such vitality in me to form relationships, to deepen my life.

Clinical Comment: In working with Jacob, I began by doing exercises to deal with his split. I intensified his rotation pattern, his avoidance stance. This stance served to return him back to childhood and to avoid facing the death of his idealized father. He had not been able to grieve and to protest his father's death and his resulting aloneness.

The shock therapy also disorganized Jacob and created confusion and tremendous rigidity as a defense against collapse. To work with this pattern required a combination of undoing his spasticity, increasing his feelings of being young and helpless, while forming a structure to contain tender and vulnerable feelings. As his rigidity decreased, he became more sure of his own manhood and he no longer had to fit his father's image.

What Somatic Education Means

When a therapist enters the somatic-emotional process of a person he encounters more than a person's ideas about himself or his habitual feeling state. He begins to discover the person's embodied history and how his interactions with himself and others creates a human shape that guarantees his tomorrow. A somatic educator also seeks to grasp the nature and the meaning of an insult and the disorganizing and reorganizing function which allows the formative process a voice, and how this voice is a connection to the individual as well as to something bigger than the individual.

That is the spirit that should underlie all somatic-emotional work. It takes courage, and awe, and wonder, on behalf of the therapist and the client, to work somatically. A somatic educator is more than a mechanic for the body or an intensifier of emotion; he is a person who works with the process of creation. To discover what this process means to the client is different than imposing a stereotyped goal upon him.

A somatic therapist seeks to learn a client's rules for forming his shape, and where, out of ignorance or fear, he abandons those rules. A person is born to create a shape, and the present moment may be the right time for him to create other shapes. This is the meaning of the statement: anatomy is destiny. Anatomy is destiny when it is seen as the ability to organize a multitude of emotional shapes. It is a negative concept when anatomy is viewed as fixed and unalterable. Anatomy is a complex morphology which manifests a particular life awareness or consciousness of sensation. A person's shape bears a direct relationship to his dimension of living. And the forming of a shape is, in fact, a destiny and a life.

There is a lot of confusion in the public mind and perhaps in the professional mind about the nature of therapy. For a long time the goal was to frustrate the person and have him solve his problems on his own. But experience shows that healing does not occur in isolation. There is a need for another who shares his experience with the client as he helps him to form his own experience. Healing requires the human voice and human interaction.

Therapists and clients alike need to broaden their understanding about what they think somatic work is. A somatic vision calls on them to be courageous in following their own processes and their own shaping. It asks them to discover how they want to organize their life and, to the best of their ability, to live it. What a person creates and forms remains with him all of his life. If one lives only, if there is nothing he participates in, he becomes passive to his existence. But if he makes the effort to form something for himself, that shape becomes his organization, body, and life. This is what embodying experience is all about.

Center For Energetic Studies

The Center for Energetic Studies in Berkeley, California, under the direction of Stanley Keleman seeks to structure a modern contemplative approach to self-knowing and living in which one's own subjective process gives birth to a set of values which then guides the whole of one's life. Today's values are increasingly divorced from our deepest processes, and bodily experience has been misunderstood and relegated to second place.

Somatic reality is an emotional reality that is much larger than innate genetic patterns of behavior. Emotional reality and biological reality are the same and cannot be separated or distinguished. Biological ground also means gender, the male and female responses that are innate to human life, the sexual identity with which we are born. Somatic reality is at the very core of existence, the source of our deepest religious feelings and psychological perceptions.

Classes and programs at the Center offer a psycho-physical practicum that brings to use the basic ways a person learns. The key issue is how we use ourselves—learning the language of how viscera and brain use muscle to create behavior. These classes teach the essential somatic aspect of all roles and dramatize the possibilities of action to deepen the sense of connection to the many worlds in which all of us participate.

For further information, write to:
Center for Energetic Studies
2045 Francisco Street
Berkeley, California 94709